GREY, Charlotte

Doon the road

D0432770

DOON THE ROAD

By the same author:

No Fancy Life, The Book Guild 2001

Tric-Trac, The Book Guild 2003

DOON THE ROAD

Charlotte Grey

Book Guild Publishing
Sussex, England

First published in Great Britain in 2003 by
The Book Guild Ltd,
25 High Street,
Lewes, East Sussex
BN7 2LU

Typesetting in Baskerville by
IML Typographers, Birkenhead, Merseyside

Printed in Great Britain by
CPI Bath

A catalogue record for this book is available from
The British Library.

ISBN 1 84624 024 7

To J. W.

Contents

Caminante,

no hay camino,

se hace el camino

al andar.
ANTONIO MACHADO

Translated: Traveller, there is no path,
the path is made by walking.

GLOSSARY

aa	all
aal, aul	old
affa	awful
ahin	behind
airts and pairts	(from) all over the place
aye	always
bawbee	small coin
bide	dwell, stay, wait
bidey-een	live-in lover
bittie	bit
bummle	muddle, mess
cauldrife	cold
chiel	man
coontin'	counting
coorse	coarse
cottar house	farm cottage
dae	do
dee	die
deen	done
deil	devil
ding	beat

dinnae	do not
doon	down
droon	drown
ee	eye
een	eyes, one
eneuch	enough
erse	arse
fae, frae	from
faur	where
fecht, fechter	fight, fighter
ferm	farm
fin	when
fit	what, foot
fou o'the fit	foot infection
gaan	going
gie	give
gied	gave
ging	go
Goldwater	Murray Gray bull
hale	whole
han-barra	wheelbarrow
hefted	attached, bonded
heid	head
hert	heart
hiv	have
hivven	heaven
hoosie	house
lang	long
lippen	trust, have faith
loon	a boy, son

loutherin'	loafing
mair	more
morn's morn	tomorrow
muckle	much, big
nae	no
naething	nothing
neiper	neighbour
on-cairry	keep on
pit	put
preen	pin
quine	girl, young woman
redd up	clear up
richt	right
roup	farm sale, auction
sair	sore
sharn	muck, manure
shooglie	shaky
sicht	sight
siller	money
skeeg	whack
snaa	snow
snorl	tangle
soor	sour
sooth	south
spik	gossip
stane dyke	dry-stone wall
steading	farm building
steek	shut

steen	stone
stracht	straight, street
stramash	fuss, bother
tak	take
tak the lift	patronise, try it on
thocht	thought
thole	bear, endure
throu-han	under consideration
trauchled	wearied, overworked
twa	two
tyauve	struggle
wark, wirk	work
warslin'	working away, struggling
weel	well
wha	who
wha'se	whose
whaur	where
widnae	would not
wint, winted	want, wanted
umman	woman
zotz	eliminate, kill

1

The Best Business

Every autumn the farm looked well. A benign light turned stubbles golden and coloured the trees, deflecting the eyes from tired pastures. A feeling of well-being came from barns stacked to overflowing, the reward of hours when muscles ached beyond bearing and the spirit flagged. At leaf-fall light paled and only the native pine offered an unchanged shape to the sky. Routine tasks were harder with snow but a setting sun crimsoning every hill gave pause. Thaw and the booming river still brought its heavy spoils to toss against the brig.

The farmhouse was improved by the Aga and a stone fireplace built to replace a commonplace tiled one. Wood gathered on their own land comforted many a quiet evening for John and Charlotte Grey as they listened to music or caught up on reading. Farm work had made them physically fit but they were undoubtedly shabby: there was little point in sprucing up when cows had no sense of timetable. At any time a strange noise would send them over to the steading: it could happen that pyjamas were worn on rescue missions, but thankfully not often.

As a new farmer reading everything that came to hand, John Grey had come across Adolphus Speed who in the year 1659 praised turnips as excellent for feeding and fattening all sorts of cattle, saying that cows fed on them gave milk with 'full vessels' three times a day throughout the year. There was

no doubt that Adolphus spoke truly, in fact cows went crazy over the turnip, ate with relish every morsel of their ration and would fight for the smallest gobbet of any other beast's share. Providing this delight brought problems that farmer Speed knew not.

John was advised to plant 'yallers' rather than the purple variety and purchased seed to be sown by a contractor with specialist machinery for the job. The date of the planting was quite late, giving plenty of time for the preparation of the land, rotavating and clearing – again, contracted work. After that it was simply a matter of waiting for the turnips to grow. Unfortunately, in the welter of green that spilled over the rows, the turnip seedlings had competition from strong and healthy weeds more likely to win any struggle to survive.

A neiper was helpful.

'Ye ken, fit ye need is a scarifier.'

John bought one to attach to the three-point linkage of his tractor; driving between the planted rows should then dislodge the weeds. It could not be said that every weed was zotzed by this useful implement but afterwards the turnips had a better chance.

A later foray between rows loosened fully-grown turnips to make collecting them easier. Pulled out of the soil, the turnip was topped and tailed by using a razor-sharp knife, the 'heuk', to remove greenery and slice off the root before throwing it into a waiting cart. Back to the steading with the load, to tip and land satisfyingly on the concrete floor of the store. Several trips would provide enough feed for a day or two but there was a limit to the keeping quality of the neeps – left too long they would deteriorate, go soft and produce an unpleasant smell. Tractor, special implements, cart, heuk and willing hands obtained this beneficial food for the good of the herd. John and Charlotte, new to the chore, enjoyed the cold clear air and the timeless feel to it, but weather could transform the task into nightmare, all movement

2

clumsy when winds whipped at the face and eyes were blinded by sleet. Then the neeps were ice, and burned at the touch. The tractor would bog down and loads slew on the way back to the steading as gateway and muddy track deepened into morass.

Through the years at Burnside they persevered but at Bithnie, with more land, more cattle and many planned improvements John gave up the struggle and replaced the turnip feed with bought-in concentrates. The rattle of these pellets in the plastic skips formerly used for neeps alerted the cows in the same way. The taste was found good, there was the same willingness to fight over them but never again were the lip-smacking juicy pleasures of the turnip witnessed. It was 'the economy stupid' in farming terms, and a pity. 'Ye ken noo John!' said other farmers who had given up on the neep.

Charlotte's reading also turned up a gem from the past, from the year 1794. In a book about early schools there was a quotation from Webster's *Little Reader's Assistant,* entitled 'Farmer's Catechism' in question and answer form. It read as follows, the text having the letter 's' written as a sinuous curve like the letter 'f' without a crossbar:

Q: Why is farming the best business a man can do?
A: Because it is the most necessary, the most helthy, the most innocent and most agreeable employment of men.
Q: Why is farming the most innocent employment?
A: Because farmers have fewer temptations to be wicked than other men. They live much by themselves, so that they do not see so many bad examples as men in cities do. They have but little dealing with others so that they have fewer opportunities to cheat than other classes of men. Besides the flocks and herds which surround the farmer, the frolicks of the harmless lambs, the songs of the cheerful birds and the face of nature's works, all

3

present to the husbandman examples of innocence, beauty, simplicity and order, which ought to impress good sentiments on the mind and lead the heart to God.

She showed this excerpt to John and studied his face as he read it. What reaction would there be? The same as her own? It would be so easy and so amusing to demolish, make smart remarks about bidey-eens or about dyke-lowpers, applying this latter term to people rather than cattle. Enough gossip surfaced in the Howe to make a nonsense of claims to a simple, virtuous life, and yet ... She waited.

'It's a bit rosy, I suppose, applied to the present day, but it is, well, nice, I really like it. Well done Mr, er, whatsisname?' Peering again at the page. 'Mr Webster!' He handed back the book. There was no doubt that Adolphus and Mr W were in their own times what folk in the Howe described as 'wise-spoken' men.

2

'... Nor any Drop to Drink.'

When did it start, the regard for cows? It was a far cry from
early childhood, John's in a city, Charlotte's with no memory
except of hurrying when a beloved dog was with her, fearful
that somewhere in the middle of grazing cows was a bull
ready to chase and gore both of them. As if from another
planet these lumbering giants were not touched, stroked or
admired at that time. Later, on a summer holiday in Wales,
she had seen fat cows with coats of a polished slaty black so
sleek she remembered the picture they made in a meadow
bright with flowers, but of course it was not a close
encounter.

When they bought the hill farm of Burnside, for a few
weeks John had to remain in England and Charlotte was left
in charge of 25 cows with calves at foot and an Aberdeen
Angus bull. Looking back brought many a rueful laugh at
her dogged patrolling, counting and miscounting calves and
cows free to wander over what seemed an enormous expanse
of land. The cows were much bigger than she had expected;
she felt dwarfed by them and fear of the bull made life
difficult. With less than rudimentary knowledge she
attempted to judge their well-being while keeping a drystane
dyke between herself and himself.

A stream on the hill dried out and animals bellowed to tell
her. She was well aware that cows needed a lot of water, had

5

read about it and witnessed the way they drank great draughts of the precious stuff. Slowly it was taken and savoured, the head back as the last drops trickled down the the throat – she found it pleasant to watch that. Across the hill, streams had bubbled through narrow channels, spilling here and there into shallows where moorhens swam. The source supplying the little streams now lay exposed, the sand pale and fissured, the pebbles without colour except where a gleam of quartz enlivened them. Where had the water gone? How could it disappear? What was to be done? A spasm of annoyance came that she was left on her own to deal with this. What would John have done? What would any of the people hereabouts do? She followed the channel to their boundary fence and looked at the dried cleft on land owned by somebody else. From the hill the miserable plaint of her cows did not lessen. Charlotte had been brought up strictly: she had never stolen anything, was law-abiding and told only small lies. Looking around she could see not the smallest sign of life. In a distant cottage people were likely to be switching on to watch *Coronation Street,* and she wished she could do the same. Instead she carefully lowered the top strand of rusting wire between leaning fence posts and began her trespass.

Hurrying, she followed the dried-up course until it ended in a tumble of heather over a stony outcrop which seemed at odds with the nature of the place. Tentatively, she moved aside some of the heather and to her surprise it was damp. There was something else, a faint sound, of water. Pushing away stones her hands became wet but there was no flow. This came when she unearthed something nasty, the sodden corpse blocking the exit. Hare or rabbit, she neither knew not cared. She watched water gather pace, flow where it was meant to flow, and followed, back to home ground. An accident or deliberate act? A natural occurrence? In her heart she knew it was not so, the poor creature had been

firmed in by clumps of grass and the stones and heather were arranged.

Long ago she and John had met a truly remarkable man who later became a Buddhist monk: they had admired the way he dealt with any problems and never forgot his reaction to an unpleasant happening. He smiled and said 'I was aware of it!' when people were indignant on his behalf. Charlotte decided not to tell John before he arrived to share all burdens: until then, she would be aware, very aware. Water was flowing and that was the main thing. She watched the cows drink before going into the house to put the kettle on.

Another trial involved water but this time too much of it. On a very hot day she found cows in what looked like a small reservoir, perhaps merely cooling themselves, but Charlotte, perturbed by the depth of water almost submerging them, and afraid small calves would follow and drown, decided to drive them out of the pool. It was not the best of ideas: exhausted, sweaty, she gave up, half inclined to join the bathers except that pushing through sheltering gorse bushes to see what all the fuss was about came the black bull.

3

All the Beasts are Mine ...

There were rewards for a trauchled beginner. Hereford-Shorthorn cows have dark red hides and creamy-white faces and at first Charlotte could not tell one from another, but slowly they took on identity: a variant of tone in the red colouring, a band of creamy-white along the spine, facial markings, perhaps a blotch of red over one eye or both, a patch on the nose, all becoming increasingly familiar as the patrols to check and double check continued. They behaved differently: a cow left with some horn after a clumsy dehorning did not endear herself; frisky and belligerent she aimed at being boss. One or two were gentle and friendly, others watchful or shy. It was inevitable that a naming process began. Time would reveal that not all the names were well chosen: a cow in a fanciful moment christened 'Comfort' because she was a splendid specimen who liked to be petted, offered none, was difficult to get in calf and not always a good mother when she did give birth. The horn-cow called Gertie developed bullying tactics undreamed of by the sweet, fussy namesake in the other life. People were not sure of honour done to them. Hearing you had a bovine identity caused odd reactions and needed confirmation – 'Oh, but she is lovely,' Charlotte would explain. 'If only you could see her. A super one she is, really, with almost perfect conformation!' It cheered her to give the impression of being knowledgeable

when every day brought truth that, in a pungent phrase from her native county, she knew 'less than a pennorth o'nowt!'

A stranger in a strange land, she gave herself a boost by naming the black bull 'St George' but did not breach distance between them or test opinion that 'a bull's best faced an'lookit i'the ee': from behind the sheltering dyke she hoped to judge his well-being. This state of affairs suffered a jolt when late one night she saw he did not put weight on a back foot. Surely she was mistaken; the light was fading and maybe the ground was uneven? She watched for a while but he grazed in the same spot, did not move very much at all. She returned to the house wondering what one did with a limping bull and was fearful of finding out. An anxious sortie at first light brought confirmation: St George was lame.

Action this day, as Mr Churchill had said. What action? Rather miserably she checked the rest of the herd and went back to make a cup of tea. She rang the vet who cheerfully told her to get the bull in and he would come and have a look. Get him in! Ah, there was the rub. A neighbour had sometimes worked on the farm for the previous owner and when she telephoned he was 'oot amang the beasts': his wife promised he would come later and bring the 'loon' to help; the 'loon' not what he sounded like to English ears, but their son.

St George proved rather a gent and came quietly. The trick was in bringing the nearest cow with him, guiding both back to the steading where Charlotte produced a morsel of hay, and the experienced Samaritan slipped a halter over the neck and secured him ready for the vet. 'Ah reckon it's fou' o'the fit' was his verdict, as they stared at the bull's broad back. 'It's nae problem, ye ken, soon sorted!'

And it was! The vet came, filled a syringe with a remedy; injected St George and went on his way promising to send a bill in due course. Neighbour accepted the offer of a dram. Loon, after a sidelong glance at his father, refused politely.

The previous owner of the farm was talked about and also criticised for ploughing a field, with the blade 'nae richt.' Charlotte shook her head wisely, while registering the fact that close scrutiny is possible over acres of land seemingly empty. New farmers would not escape.

The loon recalled one strange and delightful picture from the past. Looking for the son of the house he had gone into the steading to find him recumbent in a fourposter bed listening to the radio. Listening to what else but *The Archers* … bliss indeed!

4

Man is Born to Trouble ...

This old truth is not aimed at the 'trauchled fermer' alone, but sometimes he believes he is singled out. Always aware of a 'muckle slippy steen' at his door and suspecting that there could be 'twa o' them' his demeanour can be less than sunny.

The years at Burnside had been a learning process. In the early days they had been overwhelmed by each setback, the whole of their thinking affected and the days made miserable. With mounting problems, the only solution was containment, doing whatever they could in each case but striving to remain calm. They tried to be resilient but if they judged lack of experience had resulted in mishap to any animal they became upset and blamed themselves, refusing the excuse of occasional bad luck. One such instance at Bithnie gave much stress and extra work over many weeks. In fact, nothing ever expunged the feelings of regret and sadness evoked. It had to do with twin calves and the cow called Comfort.

It happened on a really lovely day in springtime, before the grazing was at its best. In the smaller wood and its adjoining pasture, cows decided to press for a move as cows do when they feel they have exhausted all benefit from the grass. The method of communicating is to bawl *sforzando*, to bring the farmer to investigate, follow him *sustenuto* as he walks round to check, achieving *crescendo* at the gate, the

11

message crystal clear. To ignore all this takes nerve and if another field is available the cows have won. That was the way of it when John decided to give in and move them to a small paddock which had a reasonable flush of grass. Checking for the next one to calve would be easier as the paddock was near both house and steading. It seemed to be a good idea and the very willing migrants made an easy transfer to the new park.

To get some idea of the confusions which followed this move it is necessary to refer to notes scribbled at the time, which read as follows:

April 20th	FLORA – calved 6.45 a.m. Typical Flora calf, white, stripy bull.
	LUCY – 8.45 a.m. Heifer.
	Later both calves brought to steading and Flora's trodden on but seems OK. Managed to feed them separately.
	BONNY – in wood. Heifer.
April 21st	KITTY – bull calf.
	Flora's calf confused. Put them in silage pit to bond. Later see it suck.
	Similarly Kitty, in silage pit.
	MOLLY – in wood. Calved heifer and then to our surprise another one. She eventually left the first. We get them inside. Later give artificial feed to no.1. Not good.
	GERTIE – bull calf. OK has sucked.
	DOLLY? COMFORT?
April 22nd	COMFORT restless. Went off and came back.
	Later in paddock gave birth to a dead heifer.
	Frantic licking. Anguished bawling.
	We lift the calf and she follows.
	Have to put her inside. She is in a state.
	What to do?

It was at this point that they decided on an action that proved mistaken – to give the rejected twin to Comfort. This is a normal thing – a calved cow has milk that must be drawn off or she will suffer mastitis and resultant damage to the udder. If no calf is available on the farm one must be purchased elsewhere, which carries risk: first that she will reject the substitute and second that infection might arrive with the imported animal. An alternative is to write off the loss and milk the cow daily, obviously extra work the trauchled farmer does not welcome. A cow with a strong mothering instinct will accept a substitute calf without much fuss, another might stubbornly resist or react violently simply because she knows the calf is not hers. In such a case various methods are tried, for example smearing the poor calf with detritis from the unsuccessful birth or more drastically the skin is removed from the dead calf and fitted to the potential adoptee. All the strategies are time-consuming and unpleasant in the middle of a busy time on the farm. When calving brought less serious problems which nevertheless had to be treated and involved separating a cow and calf from the main herd, John often lacked places to put them in; every nook and cranny in the steading gained occupants for special and necessary reasons. Now and again, trusted gentle animals could share the same 'cell' but with others that was something of a risk. Cows are creatures of the open air, needing to range far and wide as they graze; they do not like to be contained.

The diary tells of Comfort's reaction:

We daubed up the calf and she does not mistreat it but it is no go! She is frantic to escape. We go to check on others and do various jobs and discussing what to do remember her going off and coming back later. By the grace of God we go to the wood ...

It was there, nestled deep in long grass, the evening sun speckling its brown curly coat, a perfect small waiting calf.

5

It did not need Inspector Morse to unravel the sequence of events: Comfort had given birth in the wood, and as a creature of the herd was caught up in the clamour for fresh grass. Taken into custody after the trauma of a second birth in the paddock, she was unable to go back for number one calf. Her frantic behaviour and indifference to a substitute calf was explained.

With hindsight it was possible to see how they went wrong. Tired by dealing with several mother/calf problems all at once, and mindful of the plight of Molly's rejected twin, they decided to bring the now bewildered creature to its mother and did not take her to the wood to discover the calf for herself. They judged it better to have Comfort in the steading under control rather than allow her freedom to roam when she might or might not suckle either calf. After restoring the wood calf to Comfort, attention was diverted to Rose who eventually produced a fine bull calf at 11 p.m. 'Born in a thick cowl' reports the diary, so it was a fortunate distraction – unsupervised, Rose would have lost a very good calf. Returning later to Comfort they found her well away from both calves, showing interest in neither. This did not make for sound sleep. A note the following day reads: 'Up at 5 a.m. Comfort far from peaceful. Feed glucose drink to both calves and they go for her. Molly's succeeds in spite of kicks. Giving

15

glucose as a booster seems to work. Molly is a disturbing influence, her noises affect her calf.' Later that day: 'Adopted calf suckled. Her own is the problem.' And the day after: 'Comfort has rejected her own calf and tolerates the other. What irony! Later on we let her out and she chases foster child. Maternal is the word. We have to feed the other.'

The diary does no more than hint at the sheer grind of early rising, long busy days and late nights. A compact calving as advocated by the College was desirable in that it achieved calves of even size and weight but the policy carried a price John and Charlotte paid. To say they were tired was a massive understatement. They tried to give each other an hour's rest now and again, but what was needed was full-time help they could not afford. They used contractors for work on the land but the care of the cows was paramount and theirs alone. Thirteen calves were born at the time of Comfort's saga of misfortune and to all this stramash was added the chore of feeding the little bull calf. A quantity of milk powder was mixed to be bottle-fed, as with a small baby. This was the beginning of a long-lasting attachment between the little creature and Charlotte. She gave him the name of Mole, partly because of the colour of his hide but also she had read a story about a Miss Mole, who throughout life had been dealt the 'clorty end o' the stick': there was a parallel she thought.

One bottle, then two, three, four and eventually five bottles each feed for many weeks, the calf sucking eagerly at what was in fact a poor substitute for the real thing.

With increased growth in the parks the cows were more content and did not always return to the steading for a bite of hay, making it possible for John to give more room to young stock still housed. If it rained heavily the yearlings were returned to their original space and gates shut on them so the cows could be fed as before. Cows and calves with problems remained in their various places in and around the

steading, fed on the dwindling stock of hay and grass John somehow found time to scythe from around the buildings.

More calves were born. More problems including outbursts of really drenching rain and the consequent need for shelter. In the dry spells John managed some work on the land, spreading muck, harrowing, and Charlotte cleaned any place vacated by a treated animal to minimise risk of infection.

Mole is mentioned in the diary:

Comfort in paddock with both calves. Mole takes full bottle.
Calf fed 40 fluid ounces – 4 times daily.
RAIN. Calf fed full bottle but would not stay in!
Dried Mole off and gave extra milk as he seemed desperate.
Calf much livlier. On 10 pints a day!
Garden gate left open and calf walked into the house. Keen!
Calf not there for 9 p.m. feed. Had to climb brae to find him with herd.
Mole less eager for milk and is scouring.
Calf is scouring but drinks two bottles. Others are scouring.
Late feeding Mole. Only 3 times today as vet says 'cut down'.
Mole at far end of farm, so need long trek. Seems in good nick!
Mole – morning – stiff bowel motion: runny by evening.
Anxious for last feed so as to follow others up brae.
We see Mole 'high tailing' it with other calves!

The story continues, a see-saw of improvement, setbacks, treatment for scour, coughing, but increasing independence and integration with the herd. Mole was more affected by

heavy rain than other growing calves, and was often dried off and kept inside against his will. He is recorded as 'pathetic', 'vocal' and 'fatter'. His shape is not what it might have been, but 'stomachy', his coat patchy. However, he survived, as John pointed out to a despondent Charlotte – 'Had we not gone to look for him...' A particular entry made by Charlotte encapsulates the whole episode: 'Calf galloped towards me at 10.15 p.m. and drank avidly. Then coughed. Went up to Comfort – she nosed him but went off to find her 'own'.

6

Tiger, Tiger …

He drove slowly up the farm road and stopped in front of the steading where John was cleaning sharn from the concrete after the cows had left. He levered himself from the driving seat and came with outstretched hand and a wide smile in the natural brown of his face to greet John who, to the best of recollection, had never seen him before.

'Perhaps we'd better move away from this … er, stuff.'

John leaned against the stones of the garden wall, hoping that whatever it was it would not take long; he was anxious to finish the cleaning and go inside for the supper Charlotte would have ready.

The farm's setting, in hills bathed in benign autumn sunlight, was admired at some length and it seemed that the Bithnie cows were the finest specimens seen in all the visitor's travels. The man did not appear to be selling anything and he was smartly dressed, his vehicle a four-by-four of current registration.

'I'm sorry, Mr, er?' The name came swiftly.

'I am Sammy Sampson. Very pleased to meet you. I am visiting the old country from my home in Bombay, in India,' he offered. 'I am calling on all the farmers …' The explanation went on, his friendliness touching, like that of a young puppy, but smells from the kitchen were drifting from an open window. The smile beamed, and brown eyes grew hopeful.

19

'Do you, sir, perhaps have much game on this good place?'

So that was it. All the chat, round and round the houses when what he was after was a spot of shooting.

''Very little, Mr Sampson, and I am not keen on other people around my cattle, especially with guns: with so much stock about, it isn't good.'

'Sir, I am a very fine shot. In my country as you know, we have tigers! Big game! We know all about taking care; the animals would be quite safe around me, I can assure you.' Head back, he laughed heartily, perhaps the time spent in the forests of the night warm in recollection.

'I'm sure you are very skilled, but I'm sorry, it's no good, not here.' John turned away, ready to go back to the chore, when an eager hand touched his arm.

'You perhaps will change your mind, if I call again? I would pay, handsomely, of course?' The smile refreshed a face which had become anxious. 'I am a very, very good shot, you will see!'

'Afraid not. You could find somewhere else ...' John gestured vaguely around, 'But I must get on ...'

When at last all was shipshape and supper was in front of him, Charlotte was curious.

'What did he want? He seemed keen!' She had taken a look through the kitchen window.

'He hoped to get a shoot. Out of our league, though. He shoots tigers ... has a rug made from one he shot ... couldn't let him loose here!' He reached down to finger the ears of the gentle cat at his feet.

Mr Sammy Sampson did call again and then again, unaware that John Grey was not a man to change his mind concerning the welfare of his cattle. There was however, one quite blatant attempt to get permission to shoot. Charlotte discovered a large parcel, addressed to THE OWNER OF BITHNEY FARM AND LANDS. Inside the parcel was an overall of dark green material most surprisingly lined with

20

fur. A note read: 'Please accept this very fine suit and best wishes from your friend Sammy'. There was no address or indication how the parcel had arrived on the doorstep.

'Well, I'll be damned!' They exchanged looks. 'The beggar!' Trying to fit the suit back into its plastic bag and the brown paper wrapping, John gave an exasperated chuckle. 'How on earth can we get this back to him? No address. Nothing to say where he holes up.'

Charlotte was smiling. 'Don't worry, I fancy he'll be back. In fact I think you are being stalked ...'

They kept the parcel handy to await a visit which strangely did not come. There was however, a sequel of an unexpected kind. The Forestry Commission owned adjoining land and were planting at no great distance from the Bithnie cottar house. The woodsmen parked their vehicle in front of this cottage before trudging up the hill about their business. Often they would come down, take flasks and packages from the Land Rover, and loll around to enjoy a rest and snack meal or a smoke. John did not particularly like this trespass but tolerated it, believing it essential to keep on good terms with any neighbour or that neighbour's workforce. Passing the time of day with the men, they told him that an Indian gentleman had permission to shoot the Forestry land and was likely to be around for a day or two. They had not come across the gentleman as yet.

They did not have to wait long. As John walked off towards the steading he was startled by the sound of gunfire followed by angry yelling and many expletives. He turned to see not very athletic bodies running for shelter at a rate of knots. The exodus was necessary: jagged holes in green paintwork were proof enough of an assassin at large on Bithnie Hill. 'You know,' John said as they sat at lunch, 'I have a small doubt about that tigerskin rug!'

7

'Might I Have a Bit of Earth?'
The Secret Garden, *F.H. Burnett*

It was not so much a knock at the door, more a little scrape that could have been the grey gander demanding a slice of bread, but Charlotte asked John to attend to it. A casserole had been in the Aga while they worked in the steading and vegetables were just about ready. She waited and yes, there was talk. Not the simple need for a slice of bread then. The voice went on and on without a word from John to stem the flow. She moved the pan away from the heat: it was a nuisance, whatever or whoever it was. John would soon make excuses; their early start and hard work made a break for lunch very welcome. Now he was speaking and in response came a little gurgling laugh, a throaty very feminine sound, more drinks party than farm door. If this turned out to be a social call would there be enough vegetables? This was the time to bang on a saucepan and shout 'Come and get it', as they did in old films, but Aberdeenshire was not the Wild West. A pity but there it was. She waited. The voice was a meandering stream, briefly a pool while the other person spoke. Whatever was it about? At this time of day when they needed to eat!

It ended. Through the window Charlotte saw cows stop grazing, curious about a body different from the rag-bag outlines normally seen. She saw the person move to stroke a

broad red back and thinking of the spoiled greens wished the cow had been Gertie with the residual horn. The figure did not open or climb over the closed gate to the farm road but slipped through the bars. Neat was the word for it.

John came back to the kitchen. Like the cows he appeared confused.

'What was all that about then?'

'We … ell, nothing much really. In fact I'm not sure what she wanted.'

'It seemed to take a long time finding out!'

He became busy concentrating on the food slammed in front of him. It emerged that the visitor had called to make herself known. She was Lady X, interested in farming and the River Don. Her husband was keen on fishing, an excellent hobby because he was, to quote, 'older, well, much older'.

'And what,' Charlotte could not resist, 'is Lady X keen on?'

'Not scruffy farmers, I reckon!'

'I will deal with her when she comes again, just in case!'

It so happened that another scrabbly little knock came when Charlotte was alone in the house and John at work elsewhere. Because the day was warmer there was no furry hat but a lot of reddish hair touched the collar of a good tweed coat. A charming face was enhanced by skilfully applied make-up. Lady X queried whether Mr Grey was available but had to be content with Charlotte who, like John, became mesmerised, launching the merest ripple when Lady X's stream halted to oxygenate itself with breath or a further thought. There was no intention to interrupt Charlotte's busy life so an invitation to come inside was not accepted and both remained standing at the door. There was time to reflect that the fluting voice of Lady X was younger than her face.

Later, analysing droplets from the conversations and filtering them into a splash of probabilities, it seemed that one or both of them had given permission for Lady X to

wander at will over the farm. Never would she disturb them or be a nuisance: walking among the cattle would be happiness, she would breathe the scents, absorb all sounds, in a renewal of what she held most dear. Fences would not be climbed over. Without undoing any gate fastenings she would slip through, that was easy for her, being so small. As always when the petite point out their delicacy of build, Charlotte felt bigger, ballooned almost; average height and inability to pass through the bars of a gate were crosses to bear. Glistening above all else came a dewdrop: Lady X intended to bring Lord X to see them when she had worked on him 'a teeny, teeny bit more'. Mr and Mrs Grey would find him charming as everybody did and he would surprise them with his knowledge of simply everything. Of course Lord X gave serious thought to her own ideas; his support was always there.

It was perplexing. Charlotte and John were totally involved in running the farm, social life practically non-existent, and now this possibility of Lady X slithering neatly under gates or bobbing up in the middle of the stock. Overwhelmed, they awaited Lord X. Discreet enquiries about him yielded little except that he was a captain of industry. Another one 'frae London wi'muckle siller' but true in this case.

Charlotte heard the tric-trac of the bridge and guessed that out of the gold-coloured Rolls coming slowly up the farm road Lady X would produce the genie of her Lord and so it proved. She asked the visitors into the kitchen explaining that John would come in shortly as he would hear the bridge wherever he was working. Lady X talked with friendliness and charm, consulting Lord X, leaning over to touch his hand, smiling and prettily demanding agreement. Charlotte hoped that John would come soon. It had occurred to him and to herself that interest shown might be in Bithnie farm rather than farming generally, which would seem the most awful cheek.

24

'Be polite John, if he wants to buy us out, don't lambast!'

'Would I ever?'

'Well, it's not his fault she feels like Marie Antoinette.'

'There's a thought!' They had become entranced with the prospect of a blue and white dairy at Bithnie.

When John did appear Charlotte could not help smiling – he was not in the least bit conscious of the contrast between his clothes and Lord X's country wear. Charlotte poured coffee and then Lady X revealed her plan, not for a lock, stock and barrel purchase, but would Mr Grey consider selling the park to the left of the bridge? If they could have just a little land near to the river where Lord X could fish and she could have a little cabin, perhaps with a patio and some sort of driveway for the car …? The expression on the face of Lady X should have melted a stone.

It was then that Lord X took over. He was willing to pay a good price for the field, which he noticed needed better drainage than at present but he could see to that. If John did not want a cabin there, would he consider selling the cottar house? It was impressive, the confident offer put straight, man to man. But Lord X was quick to see the error of judgement made by his wife.

'Ah! You do not wish to sell. There is no chance …?'

'No. None at all.'

It was interesting to think of a busy Lord X taking time to humour his little wife who looked straight ahead as the golden Rolls slid away. John thought Lady X was prone to flights of fancy and would soon recover. Charlotte imagined some kind of compensation would be provided, say a necklace like the French queen's.

8

'Looped and Window'd Raggedness'
King Lear, *William Shakespeare*

John was unconcerned about appearance. In their time at Burnside, he was just a little smarter than tinkers who called at the farm now and again. So mechanical was the task of hoeing turnips that he could enjoy the day and all the burgeoning green around and about while thinking of his plans for the farm, and it had to be admitted, the rabbit pie Charlotte had made for lunch. Reverie was broken by a summons: 'Hey, you! Come 'ere!' A stout man had slammed the door of his expensive car and was leaning over the dyke. John walked slowly towards him.

'Yes … sir?' he said, touching his forehead as a token of respect. Mr Arbuckle did not see the irony.

'Some fool misdirected me. Shop down there! This ain't the bloody road I asked for. 'Ow do I get to …' He named the nearest village.

'Mmmmm!' said John.

The pause seemed to irritate.

'Wot's up with folk round 'ere? No bugger seems to know where 'e lives or where the next effing place is!'

He took an immaculate handkerchief to wipe his forehead and caught sight of a scratch on his paintwork.

'Look at tha-at!' It was almost a scream. The lady in the front seat of the car sank lower as if from blame. John turned

26

to the furious man. Succinctly he pointed out that directions given at the shop were unlikely to be wrong, adding that very clear maps existed …

'Plan better next time!' he suggested, and gave instructions on how to reach the desired place. 'You may turn in my drive half a mile further on.'

With a polite salute to the lady, John had gone back to work.

'Funny chap, that!' he said, retailing the encounter to Charlotte. 'Got himself into a wax!'

'Strange … How could anyone possibly have mistaken you …?' It was John's turn for irony.

Slide from a respectable appearance continued and not for John alone. When friends from England visited it was a revelation to Charlotte how many outfits were unpacked. Had she given the impression that farm life needed change every few hours, dresses, shoes, everything, when in fact she wore the same old things day after day and the same old things were at best nondescript? One day Angela moaned that a new sandal, a very expensive new sandal, had been ruined by walking in the fields.

'You should watch where you put your feet,' she reasoned, 'that's what cows do! Defecate a lot!'

Charlotte denied that once she had adored shopping, buying clothes. Angela remembered her at sales time buying unwisely and then tucking things away out of John's sight. But the sandal hovered between the friends, symbolising the gap between present and former life. Another friend had gossiped. From Australia an air mail letter read: 'Charlotte, I cannot believe it. Farm life may not require elegance but you with a broken zip! A safety pin holding things up? Never!' Truth will out.

In the other life John and Charlotte had taken holidays on the Isle of Wight during Cowes Week. A chandlers in the town, crowded to the gunwhales with boating stuff was a

magnet for John. Varnish, paint, brushes, tools, ropes, twine, canvas, blocks and tackle, navigation lights, Tilley lanterns and all their smells mingling ... it was a good place. The shop also had clothes for sailing people.

In Southampton one day, Charlotte became conscious of a tall man with a tanned face staring at her as she waited to be served in one of the big department stores. Slightly later, turning the pages of a book in WH Smith, she saw the man again, though he hastily glanced away as she looked up. She registered this without thinking it important, until buying coffee in a specialist shop, there he was, staring, half smiling. What on earth was it about? This time he plucked up courage and approached.

'Forgive me, I am so sorry. I am not following you, or perhaps I am!' It was disarming and he did appear to be respectable, not the type to pick up strange ladies.

Charlotte relaxed, abandoning a haughty return stare, and the explanation came.

'I am wondering, and you must think it the most appalling cheek, but my wife is desperate for one ... your coat ... it must be a Morgan?'

It was. In the chandlers in Cowes, alongside yellow oilskins and bodywarmers, near a tumble of woolly hats, sou'westers, deckshoes and Arran sweaters Charlotte had found the special coat, the Morgan. Unique, made by experts in the latest known waterproof fabric, splendidly cut with a marvellous system of pockets and zip fastenings, this was a very useful coat for anyone. And the tall man was not a white slaver looking for recruits, not a Don Juan on the prowl but a devoted husband, a 'hubby' even, wanting to buy a present for his wife. The coat had been the object of desire.

Such, at that time, had been the impact of the Morgan.

Many, many years later, Charlotte saw through binoculars two men with guns walking in a field of growing barley and set off to turn them away. The men did not seem concerned

28

at her approach and waited, making no attempt to slink off. With difficulty it was explained they were members of a shoot organised by the Forestry Commission for French sportsmen: the rest of their party were ... they had gestured vaguely towards Bithnie Hill and shrugged expressive Gallic shrugs with lifted brows and sad eyes and a downward twist of the mouth. They were elderly and did not want to climb ... The trespassers were invited to the farmhouse for coffee.

When all chores were done *Carmen* was Charlotte's choice of music. Sung in French it seemed appropriate. The recording had Conchita Supervia as Carmen, her wonderful mezzo-soprano voice, almost contralto in its lower range, was perfect for the role. A sumptuous, highly dramatic performance. Never to be forgotten Carmen's contemptuous rejection of Don José – '*Entre nous deux, tout est fini*' – before the fatal knife. Reliving the day, Charlotte thought of the trespassers. As they tried to communicate she noticed one of them looking at her coat ... had disdain flickered in those world-weary eyes? At first she had not registered as the owner wanting to remove them from her field of barley. Was it the coat with its broken zips and torn pockets, the worn patches at shoulder and elbow, a sagging lining? The coat not quite *de rigueur*? Still under the influence of Carmen but with some regret she decided that between her and the Morgan all was finished: tomorrow she would bin it.

9

Changeling

'I suppose it's the same as with human beings, you never can tell!' Charlotte was thinking about an incident with visitors who had just left the cottar house. They were friends who were interested in the decision to farm, kept in touch and came frequently to Burnside and to Bithnie, though it meant a long journey and an expensive overnight stop to make it bearable. The family loved the summer beauty on the farms, the hills and green spread of pasture: they wanted to hear about winter and how John and Charlotte coped in the deep snow. This support was balm when the venture had met criticism from friend and stranger alike, the latter evidenced by local opinion that John needed his 'heid examin't'.

Don involved himself in farm work to the point of exhaustion, handling hay bales, and provided the extra hand John so often needed. He knew about electrics and was invaluable when the overhead cables were replaced. His wife and daughter helped when they could and were enthusiastic about the new life. At Bithnie they climbed the braes, explored every path, discovered the chasms and dampness of the wild wood and its unexpected flowers. On the hottest days they rested, perhaps dreamed time away watching the sunlit water and the insects speckling shallow pools at its edge as the river dawdled its way to the bridge and beyond. Doreen and Debbie walked with Charlotte when she went to

look at the cows. She explained why they patrolled so often, what she looked for or feared – for example, signs of mastitis. One or two cows seemed to stand out, became recognisable, achieved celebrity status because of the tales Charlotte told. It helped to know that Lucy was willing to raise a damp, soft nose to be petted but it was wiser to step around Gertie as she did not care for familiarities. Many photographs were taken, especially of small calves with their long-lashed eyes and charming looks. It was agreed that cows could teach human beings a lot about being good mothers. As Charlotte talked to Goldwater or an Angus bull the visitors would hang back, which Charlotte well understood though she pointed out that Goldwater was something of a gent and most unlikely to be obstreperous with Bithnie guests.

Now and again the family went off sightseeing to the places everyone knew about: Fort George, Inverness, Perth, Aberdeen of course. They went north to the coast, down the steep hill to tiny secluded Pennan with its sheltering bay and minute cottages; were drawn to castles within reach of Bithnie, Crathes, Craigievar and farther away to ruined Dunottar. Longer trips took them south to Elie, famed for golf and sailing; to St Monans and an empty harbour where once fishing boats jostled close; Crail they found charming but not quite of today; Pittenweem with many boats supplied the country's fish but Anstruther's long street had provided good fish and chips. Homeward via St Andrews, its ancient university and buildings and predilection for golf. Scotland was lovely and rewarding to them but always on return Debbie said the farm was best, mooching around and looking at the cows, that was what she liked, the favourite thing.

Farm work for Don and some mooching seemed to be the pattern, repeated in the visits until a recent change. When Charlotte said, 'I'm off to see the coos. Coming?' there was hesitation, and halfway through the tour Doreen would

decide she had better go back to see how Don was and perhaps make him a cup of tea. Other things had sudden priority, a trip to the village shop or a need to tidy the cottage. So the cows had fewer visits: mooching had lost savour. Inevitably the honesty of a child yielded an explanation: Charlotte still asked the question and one day the answer came: 'Mum's a bit scared now since we got chased but I would like to come ...' Charlotte was dumfounded. 'Chased! You were chased?'

'Yes. A black one, it was. We had to run like mad!'

A flash of a smile, half gleeful. 'It was very scary! We couldn't stop shaking when we got out! We hid for ages thinking she might jump the wall and follow us.'

'But which cow? Black? One of the Angus cows?'

It dawned that excuses had always concerned the checks on the mini-herd kept separate from the others.

The mystery had to be solved. With great difficulty Doreen was persuaded to go up the brae to where peaceful black beauties grazed with a villain in their midst.

'Debbie shouldn't have told you! I didn't want to make a fuss when you're so busy!' Doreen was embarrassed, laughing now at the thought of the whirlwind flight but wary still. They walked together, spending time as usual with each animal. When Eva Jan began to call in the urgent, rather desperate way of a good mother cow, she was ignored as her calf was having fun testing strength, pushing and shoving similar wee bodies, more independent as they grew. Charlotte went to shepherd the calf back to mama and momentarily Doreen was alone ... at the speed of light from a cluster of black hides shot a black bullet doomed to miss target because at a similar speed Doreen was away over the nearest gate.

Early in the years at Burnside, after prolonged rain, an accident happened to a small heifer calf. Hour after hour entangled by roots the poor creature had hung upside down

over a crumbling wall that once shored up an avenue of trees. Very little life remained when John found her. The rescue action involved saws and an axe for the roots, sacking to protect the calf and a crowbar to prise stones from the old wall. Charlotte and John were weary and soaked to the skin when finally the calf was freed and a vet arrived. His verdict had been clear: the calf was finished; he advised John to cut his losses. Stubborness of character in both new 'fermers' rendered the idea impossible. Somehow or other they were going to save that calf: the faint spark of life had to be kindled. They isolated calf and mother cow and watched as she straddled the calf and as if by a miracle it managed to suck when John clamped its jaws over a teat. Weeks followed. The mother went back to graze with the herd, returning always to feed the calf which, though normal to look at, did not move an inch, the poor legs were useless. John decided to move her out into the sunshine, ensconced her on a pile of straw and carried her back into the steading for the night hours. So, seriously embarrassing as a lost cause and labour intensive, the little calf toyed with grass cut specially to tempt her, slept, sucked, gained a little weight and surveyed a sunlit world like a nesting swan.

There was eventual triumph when one day she did not need to be carried to her nest but got there by a painful dragging process which opened wounds for Charlotte to bandage again. Nevertheless this lifted the spirits of all concerned. It could not be said that progress was rapid. It tested Charlotte when her careful bandaging was just as carefully unpicked in the long sessions on the nest. The battle of wills was unsolved when the wounds healed. The happy ending to this part of the story came when an undersized black calf with a few white markings and a bit of a limp rejoined her mother and the herd.

The saga did not end there. This calf could not be sold when the time came and remained on the farm. Weaned and

separated from the mother she was kept with the few pure Angus cows, to a casual eye not very different from them. Fated to surprise them, she was found to be in calf, the only casualty when a rambler left open a gate and one of the bulls ambled into forbidden territory. She gave birth to a tiny slip of a calf and was in fact a born mother, proving it again and again. She repaid all the time and effort spent on her rescue. Pointed out as rather special she was loveable and friendly, an icon in her own way.

Imagine the shock horror of finding this animal to be the chaser, the stalker, villain of the piece so far as Doreen and Debbie were concerned. They had been in too rapid flight to notice the white markings, thus prolonging mystery and casting doubt on Emma-Jan, on Charity, and other blacks of a slightly temperamental disposition. Yet had the truth emerged earlier, Charlotte would have found it hard to believe. Impossible! Not that wee cow! A pause for thought. Why single out Doreen, someone kindly disposed towards all creatures including black cows? Had she worn anything, a shady hat or something strange to the cow? There can be sudden antipathy to television faces, particularly those of politicians, but between people and cows that seemed unlikely. John and Charlotte, the source of food and the only familiars? Defence of the *querencia*? But that cow! The rescued soul who thwarted death, avoided the mart and insinuated herself so cleverly into the breeding herd and rhythms of the farm. As Charlotte remarked, you never can tell …

Wullie, doing a job for them on the farm, offered the usual pungent opinion: 'It's aye weel-hid, bit ye'll nivver ding the deil oot o a 'umman or a coo!'

10

Hivven Sent!

The news that Jamie was to be married filtered through the
Howe in the usual way without money being wasted on postage
stamps or an announcement in the *Press and Journal*. Of course
there had been talk and still more when the housekeeper
arrived to look after him and the bairns. Yes, plenty of talk
against the flighty wife with Jamie certainly as the injured
party: his taciturn manner and the long hours he worked did
not excuse taking off into the Spanish sunshine with a fertiliser
rep. A former close friend received a card from Benidorm and
a later one saying they had an executive flat in East Kilbride,
which must have been a nice change after the farmhouse:
there are tiny kitchens in such flats because executives go out
to eat and this would suit Morag who was never a dab hand
except with the frying pan. Perhaps due to lack of space the
postcards did not mention any remorse, or hint at an
overwhelming passion, which was disappointing. The wee boys
and four-year-old girl had been showered with sweeties until
people forgot and other small tragedies intervened. No way
could Jamie work at the contracting which was his livelihood
and look to the needs of his family though they adapted,
becoming self-sufficient beyond their years. Getting a
housekeeper was a good solution. Few women applied for the
job. Farm life does not appeal to everyone: when winter closes
in and roads are snowbound and treacherous there is only the

fireside – cinema, disco or bingo hall are not on offer. One lady turned back before tackling the muddy road to Jamie's door. Another telephoned to say she could not take the job as she was going to Australia. The children set their faces against an elderly lady who asked too many questions and preferred bed-times much earlier than their father allowed. Another sharp-faced one offended Jamie by looking into cupboards and rolling her eyes upwards at what she saw, sniffing when he tried to explain. Then Netta turned up.

Do guardian angels exist? Are they hovering about waiting for evidence of real need? Did it register somewhere in the clouds that farm children ate pork pies and oven chips with a sticky sprawl of baked beans as a change from oven chips and eggs, sausages or fish-fingers? Was it on record that the elbows of those same farm children were poking through jumpers which were too small anyway and now and again two boys did not bother to go to the school? The answer must be affirmative because Netta was the perfect solution. Not of course quite perfect, which might have been irritating, but she took the little brood under her wing and as eventually proved was willing to shelter Jamie also. What Netta's circumstances were before she arrived at Jamie's door was unclear and attempts to gain information failed, for Netta was not talking. Smiling and with a natural courtesy she deflected all queries. The blether was she was 'frae somewhere i'the sooth', might even have been English though she never admitted it. People got used to seeing Netta shepherding the children to school: it was different for the boys with a good breakfast inside them and wrapped warm, truant days forgotten, they began to make progress. For so long dependent on not-so-willing helpers the little girl had been silent with a resigned, pale look about her but now smiles were frequent as she skipped along, her hand in Netta's. It was there for anyone to see, Netta with her good sense and kindness picking up the pieces of Jamie's shattered life to make a family.

36

The wedding took place in the register office in Aberdeen with Jamie's brothers the only witnesses apart from the boys and the tiny girl who had a pretty new frock and a small posy like Netta's. Afterwards everyone was invited to a party at the village hall, built to commemorate the proud sacrifice of the laird's sons in the Great War. Charlotte and John were invited because they had been helpful in writing to the solicitor for Jamie when he sought divorce from Morag. It was the usual affair with a good deal of happy drinking, though rules laid down by the laird specifically banned alcohol from the premises. A gentleman can conceal a bottle on his person though it does not get him on a 'best-dressed' list. The boot of a car holds plenty bottles and even a few tumblers for ladies who fuss. Jamie had arranged for a group to play for dancing and a local caterer provided food. Netta proved a good hostess, making sure that everyone had plenty to eat and knew where to find the thirst-quenchers. She had given thought to her appearance, getting a good haircut in Aberdeen, and bought a new suit and an evening dress. At the ceremony the smart suit was just right and at the party the vivid dress with a low neckline and a slit reaching above the left knee transformed Netta. People noticed a rare smile on Jamie's face as he watched his new wife doing her stuff among the guests: the guardian angels had done well. They had not however quite finished, having decided with perhaps a touch of humour to make the picture complete.

Did Jamie have a moment of perception when it came to choosing a name for the baby? He liked the children's choice but insisted on a second name so the baby was christened 'Annette Angela'. Of course Netta made a splendid mother as proved from the moment she walked into Jamie's life. There was comment about the date in the births column of the *Press and Journal* but it was good-natured; most people said, 'Wha's coontin?'.

11

Feast and Famine

Before the farming life Christmas had started early. Charlotte loved to decorate the old house, which lent itself very well to swathes and garlands and real holly taken from the orchard at the last moment. Tradition was well observed by a decorated tree with presents carefully chosen and beautifully wrapped, something Charlotte was good at and enjoyed doing. Lights in garden trees, a wreath on the door and of course a party. Logs burning in the wide fireplace John had discovered behind a Victorian one, abundant food and drink. Plenty of choice in the food – a roll of sirloin, ham, sausage to slice and mini-ones on sticks, salamis, chicken, a large stand pie, paté, quiches, anchovy eggs, salad. Cheeses, Derby Sage because of the colour, a Stilton, a creamy Wensleydale sent as a present. Olives, pickles and bread rolls. No room for sweet things on the big table, a lesser one for trifles, sponges, mince pies and biscuits and the Christmas cake, always home-made. Guests welcomed in the hall, sent upstairs to leave coats, go to the kitchen for drinks then to the sitting room but chairs have been removed so they stand to talk. As all the friends arrive a buzz of talk hits the ceiling, tells the hosts that it will be a good, successful party. A cry at the *mélange* of smells when the dining room door is opened: more wine, a plate to collect and fill, Christmas under way. To avoid trouble from breathalysers a

quantity of soup waits in the kitchen for guests who have to drive, locals who have no wish for soup steer for the gate, turning to shout Happy Christmas or something like that …

The pattern was not the same at Burnside or at Bithnie: each year Christmas seemed to swoop down on them, so things were done in a rush or not done at all. Formerly by September catalogues came in the post, newspapers advertised, shops made one aware and there was leisure to prepare. Not so on the farms – the catalogues did not find them, a newspaper was as rare as a shopping expedition. The time snatched to write cards was necessary with friends so far away but purchases were hurried and fewer. There was an obvious change of emphasis, work did not lessen because animals do not know about holidays and they came first. It sounds miserable, a diminished reaction to Christmas, when except for the holly wreath on the door decorations remained packed away and there was no thought of a party. Yet getting the work done efficiently before relaxing with a drink had its own satisfaction. Things were scaled down, quieter, but not miserable. Hogmanay promised more but Charlotte and John never acquired the stamina for embracing it as the Scots did whether they had farms to run or not.

However, one Christmas at Bithnie was memorable as a poor, lost Christmas, one that did not happen at all. In a last minute rush the Land Rover clattered the planks of the bridge with Charlotte and John bound for Aberdeen, 30 miles away, the only place for supplies for the farm, and a supermarket. Charlotte had made a list which to her secret shame included 'M&S Christmas cake' a bought cake, the first ever, and also mince pies. John would not grumble, she was the one with a compulsion to provide home baking, but crises on the farm had left no time. Hard work gave the need and the excuse for eating a lot, refuelling John called it, but she was unsure about bought stuff, could not imagine buying

a ready-made Yorkshire pud for example, though some people did.

Shopping for farm items was easy with folk at the farmers' co-operative full of good cheer and John muttered 'Too early!' to Charlotte. They did not feel festive. Crowded aisles in Asda did not help: people looked harassed, raiding the shelves as if life depended on it. Charlotte noticed a woman elbowing her way to get served at the cheese counter; the same woman allowed her two boys to dart about and get under people's feet when they rushed back to tell their mother what they liked and she must buy. Oh well, Christmas was the excuse. Not for John though, without troubling to lower his voice: 'Those little sods need a clip over the ear!' Aggrieved looks all round made Charlotte hang back though she agreed with him. Tired, with an aching back and conscious that the place was overheated, she wanted out.

The Land Rover was icy, metal took a time to heat up, and it would have been nice to travel faster. It was dark by the time they clattered the bridge again. In the steading the bunt* would be in action, the animals hungry and jostling each other not unlike the Asda shoppers. Rapid change of clothes, boots on and into the steading at a rate of knots. Afterwards the sort of peace which someone witnessing a feed had described as 'like in a church'. Booty for the house retrieved and packed in fridge or freezer, farm stuff left in the Land Rover until needed. A cup of tea next, any jostling for food could wait.

Dragging herself out of bed next morning was difficult for Charlotte: the wallpaper made her feel worse than usual and she still had backache. We have to get rid of those roses, she thought, without hope because wishing did not do the trick. John was already up and had put the kettle on but strangely he was leaning against the Aga and the face he turned towards her was haggard.

*See opening paragraph, chapter 14

'I feel bloody awful! Dizzy, and I think I'm going to be sick…' He went to the bathroom and coming back sat down, plainly shattered.

'Go back to bed!' Charlotte ordered, and was faintly surprised that he obeyed, stumbling as he went. Nothing for it then but to get going.

In the steading the cows were round the feeders tearing at hay from big bales John had manoeuvred into the rings the previous night, difficult with cows around as he worked but paying dividends now, especially with only one doing the feed.

She cut the tow from bales ready for the weaned calves and fed the hay into racks made specially by the Monymusk Lad.* They were a boon – neither young stock nor grown animals could have reached the original troughs without the court full of muck, fine when dry but unspeakable otherwise. Next the yearlings, more difficult because their housing was in a former silage pit, solid, heavy gates again from Monymusk penned them in. She checked all water troughs and was thankful there was no sharn to clear as often happened when cows performed too near. Magnesium powder replenished in the containers and she was finished, 'Aa's deen!' as Wullie would say. She had not dared to feed beet nuts to the cows, missing just once would not hurt and the job was easier with two people.

It was dismaying that John seemed no better for the lie in and did not want anything to eat which was a rarity. She made a cup of tea and toasted bread on the hot ring of the Aga. Plenty of butter and a dollop of marmalade and time to plan what to do next. It was a pity but she still felt muzzy and seemed to be getting a sore throat.

She went over again to put bales ready for the late feed. Unfortunately most of the cows lingered, only one or two

*Bill Cobban, master blacksmith based at Monymusk

had gone to the braes searching for the tasty bite that could not be there. Considerable inroads were made on the big bales and she would have to add a couple of small ones to each ring, but given early this would vanish like snow in summer and the cows on the braes would miss out. All seemed well but, turning quickly at the sound of a scuffle amongst the calves, she felt dizzy and had to grasp at the cold metal of the gate until the feeling passed. It was then she remembered it was Christmas Eve. Cold air from the doorway made her shiver in spite of being hot and sweaty from lifting bales. Going into the house she found John huddled into several layers of work clothes and quite motionless. He was staring at his boots as if puzzling how they fitted onto feet.

'You look like a deathshead moth,' she said faintly. A hood fringed with rabbit fur framed his face and had half-fallen back. Deep sunken eyes tried to focus on her. Pupation was not far off.

Between them they managed the next feed, and the next, and Christmas Day went by. They took it in turns to rest. Always the bed seemed clammy and the sheets needed changing but neither could bother. It was sufficient to lie with eyes closed against the light. Sometimes they slept. The day after Boxing Day a Range Rover pulled up outside the steading. Stuart, in Barbour and weather boots was better than Santa Claus. Sizing up the situation he lent a welcome hand. It was an immense relief to Charlotte when he climbed to get hay bales from the high stacks: she had dreaded the ladder and the height, and falling would have left a problem. Heather rang offering help and asked about Christmas dinner. Charlotte made a vague answer and it was not until later that the truth surfaced. In the kitchen, alongside mugs of cold tea, were, two plates, one with a mangled bread roll, the other with half of a sardine.

12

Erse Over Tip

Waiting to unload extra straw purchased by John, the man seemed surprised to see a woman wheeling a barrowload of muck. Perhaps the spik about rich folk frae Lunnun had reached him and Charlotte, more than a little dishevelled, did not fit his idea of a lady wife.

'Hard wirk's nae easy!' he volunteered.

'Nope!' Charlotte disposed of the muck and came back to the cart.

'Ye like it fine, then, on the ferm?'

'Yes. We do. It's great.'

Without hurry he walked into the steading, sizing up the improvements made to the old building, the weaned calves gated off, big hay bales in ring feeders ready for the cattle.

Smoke?' he proffered a packet.

'No thanks.' And firmly, 'Neither will you, not in here.'

After a second, he put the cigarettes away and began to loosen the ropes holding the bales on his cart.

It would fuel more whispers – 'Kin' o' bossy!' … 'Wears the breeks' … 'Gied me a tellin' … and she could not care: it was daft to light up with hay and straw around, fire was a hazard they could do without. She remembered John telling her that once in the Service he came across men assembling small mines actually throwing the parts to one another while

43

someone standing nearby lighted up a fag. Bossy-boots or not, smoking was out.

A friend asked, had they known all the ins and outs, the things that happened to cattle, their ills and their cussed behaviour, the horrible winter weather, would they still have done it, moved to Scotland and pursued the dream?

It had made them consider, remember and laugh, and sometimes almost weep about the troubles, the times they landed in the sharn; in Charlotte's case literally. Exactly that.

It began when a cow gave birth to a weak calf which did not survive and they needed to act quickly to find a substitute rather than take on the chore of daily milking. Each herd developed its own immunities, therefore buying in carried the risk of differing infections and they bought only when there was no alternative. This time he was a Belgian Blue, seemingly sturdy calf who proved to be a very expensive alternative, not placid as judged but sickening for a mysterious something from which he languished and finally died, though not before every calf on the farm was infected to a greater or lesser degree. A nightmare stretch of days followed when things looked black, as if the whole crop of calves would be lost. The mind became wonderfully concentrated: the calves had to survive and by all the saints they would; a syringe the weapon, brandished like the sword, primed, ever ready. Oddly the routine established again invoked Mrs Beaton and her invaluable admonition, first catch your … calf. It was beyond belief that sick, miserable scoorin' beasties were capable of such violent resistance. At an approach they ran, dodged, doubled back and when caught found demonic strength to avoid the healing touch.

After chasing, wrestling and dosing, clearing up began and went on and on, showing no sign of ever coming to an end. Sharn there was. Sharn. Not solid. Yellow, sticky, slippery, all pervasive. Concrete standings had to be cleared, washed and disinfected.

''Tis dreich wark!' observed postie, when neither of them could handle the letters he brought. 'A'll jist pit 'em i'the hoosie fae ye.'

And Charlotte's nemesis? A topper people thought before he was stricken, Sophie's calf. She found him in a corner of the steading, head down, watery yellow gunge pouring out of him, his coat matted. Not a pretty sight.

'Over here,' she called. 'Sophie's!'

Did the calf picture John approaching with raised syringe, as the Grim Reaper? At the speed of light he butted past Charlotte and was away, heading for the door and freedom. But Charlotte was practised and no slouch. She was after him, managed to head him off towards a wall where she could with luck hold him for the dose. At the wall they paused. Charlotte, closing in, attempted to smother him against the stones, to cover and hold for the needle. It was not on. In a desperate twisting movement he broke from arms coiled around his neck and was away again. Charlotte was not giving up, not by any means, but lurching after the dancing dervish was her undoing. She slipped, staggered, lost her footing and went with a squelching, shuddering thud full length into the sharn. John, aghast, saw an apparition get to its feet: little of the original was there, obscured by the obnoxious gunge that characterised their days. A woolly hat had fallen off and strange hair dripped, paws wiped at the eyes, a mouth spat words as well as other foulness. The apparition saw John ... and was it possible that he was trying not to laugh? Drawing itself up to its not very imposing height, it spoke, full of bane.

'Don't!' it said. 'Just don't you dare!'

Through the garden gate, kicking off boot, the other was in the muck. Coat, jumper, trews and the rest hurled to the path. Acting as if in a cold fury, this stripper lacked saucy, indolent moves, revealed very little pink as it stalked into the house and headed for the bathroom.

Eventually Charlotte saw the funny side of it but John was sworn to silence – there were enough rumours about folk frae Lunnun.

13

Benisons

The grey cat came into the kitchen and laid a gift at Charlotte's feet. As always the gift was a very small mouselike thing, and she knew it resulted from a patient vigil, his daily wait by a little hole no bigger than a tenpenny piece at the edge of a path near the steading. The other cats did not or dare not visit this place, which was Grey Boy's; its rewards were his alone – pale, whiskery things, skinny because they did not live to fatten themselves on oddments falling from goose or cattle feed or from the natural bounty of the land. Two things were puzzling: first the endless supply emerging to meet a grey nemesis; second, why did Grey not eat them? His vigils were lengthy, early and late, crouching in the long grass, hunched, watchful, not distracted by anyone who happened to pass and stopped to ruffle his soft fur: 'What, you there again? Come away, boy, leave them alone.'

Ignored until a crinkling nose peeping out to sniff the air brought the pounce, quick kill and delivery as usual. It was the way of things. Charlotte solemnly thanked Grey Boy and waited until he settled to sleep in his favourite chair before lifting the lid of the Aga for the cremation: it was patently unfair that the life expectation of Bithnie shrews was so brief.

On that day there was hardly any wind. The parched winter look had gone from the grass, larches on the braes showed the delicate swathes of green that began their

47

summer dressing. Patrolling the cows she found all well and there remained some time before John would come in for a meal. So unusual, an oasis of quiet with no need to rush or try to be in two places at once. The house never got sufficient attention, but household things could wait. Like the grey cat, she had earned a rest.

All three pet cats had adapted to a life very different from a rather pampered existence previously. Grey Boy had a strange start but afterwards developed fine silk fur and a plume of a tail which had to be seen to be believed. Disposed on a blue velvet cushion, the tail elegantly curled, admirers were ready to adopt him had it been decided he was too splendid to be transported to the wilds of Scotland. His story began when John heard faint scampering noises and became concerned that mice, rats or squirrels were at large in the old house. Nothing was to be seen in the attics and they forgot about the noises until they were loud and definite, causing John to get the ladder and go into the space above a bathroom. All became quiet. He came down and sat on the edge of the bath, trying to puzzle what the noises were and why they had stopped. Within seconds, descending the ladder in one lithe movement, came a black cat who shot down the stair and out through the open front door.

'Well, I'm damned!' said John. 'How in the name ...?'

He took down the ladder and went to tell Charlotte.

It was disconcerting that when he returned to remove the ladder he heard faint mewing.The black cat had in her trespass delivered herself of a kitten or kittens.

Another foray revealed a crack in the lining of the roof and by the look of it this was where the cat made her exit. Behind the lath and plaster any little mewing thing or things had not been bold enough to follow mama. Widening the crack did not help: the response was retreat along the length of the attic further away from rescue. John had no alternative but to hack at the plaster making holes big enough to tempt

an exit and Charlotte put a saucer of milk near the holes, but it was no good – as long as anyone remained in the attic the quarry kept hidden. A different strategy was needed.

On the landing between two attics was a compartment housing a large tank, and at each side of the tank there was a space big enough for a very small body to get through. Neither of them qualified and they knew of no one likely to allow even a willing child to venture through the dust and debris of years; the lath and plaster lining spoke of great age. The outlook for the litter was grim. At the time no one bothered to speculate how the black cat got into the attic: afterwards it was said that the lady she belonged to was a dab hand at getting rid of kittens and the cat was clever … an open door, access upstairs, the tank compartment door easy to open, and there was a maternity ward, ready and waiting.

The grapevine went into action. A friend of a friend had a guest, a tiny Japanese girl visiting from her home in Canada, and this girl was a good sort. In the local baker's someone reported that Yana had pointed to some particularly nice-looking cakes asking 'What are they called?' 'Oh, those ones? They are Japs!' was the unthinking answer and Yana had laughed, not minding at all.

So, with hair covered and in an old tracksuit the good sort squeezed through the space near the tank, wriggled and squirmed along, following two black kittens, although she could not see they were black at the time, eventually to catch and push them through a hole into the waiting hands of John and Charlotte. It was a cause for celebration and also for a good bath when the heroine emerged, covered from head to foot in cobwebs and plaster and dust and much else.

Charlotte prepared the bath, poured in some perfume and produced soap of rare quality. The relief was over-whelming: the two kittens could be found good homes, a sad fate avoided. Laughing and refreshed Yana accepted the offer of a drink. John went to collect the ladder and … you

have guessed, heard something. He could hardly bear to report to Charlotte and the sweet-smelling Yana, busy drying a mass of blue-black hair. It has to be said that she was made of stern stuff. Into the dusty clobber again, hair swathed, to repeat the painful progress this time to capture, yes, Grey Boy, bigger and stronger than the black kittens, cleverly avoiding capture, unaware that it was rescue. There was no question that he should be found a home. He had decided to live with John and Charlotte Grey. There was no denying it was appropriate.

14

Not With a Whisper

When cows first come together they decide the order of precedence which will govern life as a herd. Aggressiveness or fighting establishes who is the boss, the second boss and so on down the line to the last poor cow who is the bottom of the pile. Each animal will be submissive to the ones above in the social order and dominate those below. Once this is settled, peace reigns for the most part; only now and again will a challenge arise. This ordering of affairs is known as 'the bunt'. It is not on record anywhere that a herd can gang up to bully the farmer, as John found to his cost in the saga of Comfort and the twin calves. However, cows can make a considerable hullaballoo and even the hardest heart is affected when the concerted voice of all his animals is telling him they have had the best of grazing in a field and want somewhere better. He is left in no doubt. If he has no new grass to offer he skulks off, ashamed that he cannot oblige.

So he needs grass, good grass and plenty of it to maintain the health and well-being of his herd. Government subsidies are paid and accepted for re-seeding old pastures and also for reclaiming scrubland which is a much more difficult undertaking.

Re-seeding. In early years John employed contractors to do this but later shared more of the work. The process begins with the monotonous to-ing and fro-ing of a tractor with a

plough blade tearing at the old grass. Seagulls wheel and swoop round the machine but the driver cannot hear them or the steady thump of the diesel engine because music from earphones solaces or deafens him according to choice. At day's end he climbs down stiff-legged and the scent of the brown earth is refreshing. It satisfies perhaps some atavistic need he could not put into words. He is proud of the straight furrows which set the pattern for his next day's work and perhaps the next. Later the plough is changed for an implement with row on row of sharp circular discs for breaking up the heavy sods turned over by ploughing. Lime to enrich the soil is often applied then and the discs are used again. After that a harrow is dragged over from every angle, the chains ironing out any bumps to make a good level surface. A special drill is brought in to place and firm-in selected seed. A last effort with very heavy rollers leaves a smooth, blank expanse which will soon give a greening and later a flourish of new grass. As the seedsman moves off the field all birds show interest; flocks of pigeons appear as if by magic.

Scrubland with coarse grasses, clumps of reeds, gorse and whins is hard to reclaim. Often the land is steep with only a thin covering of soil. Hour after hour work goes on to fill carts with the debris of it. Roots keep a stubborn hold in the soil and many stones surface and need removing. The stone-picker can believe he is in the Gobi Desert but his stones are carted off, not used for beds or cooking. All of it is back-breaking work akin to slave labour: the motivation is the demand made by hungry mouths for pastures new. Drastic action is called for when stones are rocks or boulders of some size. If one is unearthed where it will be a nuisance in future operations it has to go. In such a case John came once more in contact with explosive materials.

The Agricultural Training Board offered every kind of help. Angus there always knew the right person. So it was that early one morning seven men, strangers to one another,

Angus and the chosen instructor met up on a northern hillside. The chill was still on the land as they climbed towards an imposing house belonging to a laird who wanted his boulder removed the expert way. A curtain moved as they passed and a woman with long black hair stared out. A little dog in her arms yapped and kept on yapping at the trespassers. A very large boulder dominated a newly-ploughed field close by.

The instructor was Thomas Cairns, a large man with sandy hair and a complexion speaking of many hours in the open air and quite a few inside a public house. He began by searching the great boulder for a likely crack or hole into which he could place gelignite. He had a licence allowing him to store this dangerous substance and he stressed the need for care.

'It's nae stuff te mess wi', ye ken.'

All were agreed on this point. Thomas got to work on the boulder with hammer and chisel and achieved a hole deep enough for the explosive. He then placed one end of a length of fuse lead into a small metal detonator and very carefully indeed squeezed gelignite around it before placing the detonator in the prepared hole. Everyone then walked back 30 yards or so. Thomas took matches from his pocket. Angus and John exchanged looks.

'Should we nae ging a wee bittie ...' The question sprang from a nervous looking farmer and someone else broke in, 'Ye ken, the hoosie's affa near ...'

Quite right. Close enough for the yapping to pierce the ear. The woman seemed not to mind.

Thomas did not move. He gave a look, smiled a pale smile that told of mastery of a craft and contempt for those who did not know what he knew.

'Na, Na, ye're a'richt faur ye are. Nae problem.'

He applied the match and all eyes followed the spark stuttering towards the boulder ...

An almighty blast ... A rending of earth, sky and probably the waters of the North Sea ... John transported back into wartime in the RN felt an urgent desire to shout 'ALL GUNS' CREWS LIE DOWN!' as rocks powered overhead and fell. Fragments large and small blackened the vault of Highland heaven. Any command would have been unnecessary – to a man the team had flattened, cowered, bitten the dust, hands shielding each ignominious head. Flat they remained for some time after the avalanche stopped.

There was not much chat as they passed the house on the way down to cars and Land Rovers. If for a moment a sly little smile hovered, Thomas kept his thoughts to himself. The nervous man became voluble, complaining to Angus who listened politely. Angus and John were the last to leave.

'The lassie at the window got a few grey hairs!'

'And the dog, it shut the yapping little bastard up!'

15

The Pain of a New Idea

They watched from the steading while the heavens opened on hay ready for the baler. They had worked late to get the field rowed up after long hours with the turner tossing and lifting to get air into the stuff, bringing it to perfection. It had looked well, fluffed high, row on row sentinel in the loury dusk. A weather forecast had been doubtful but with luck they could have baled. There was no luck.

Wullie had words for it: 'It's a bugger John. Jist shitin' doon! Jis' that!' And Wullie was right. This was not a shower of rain but full-blooded downpour to spell disaster. The quality of the hay would suffer and nothing could be done about it.

'We'd better go in. There'll be a cuppa, or a dram, maybe?'

'Ay, fairly that!'

In the afternoon the farmer contracted to bale the hay, rained off this and any other job, arrived at Bithnie. The rain drummed its certainties on the kitchen window, mocking gloom and the desultory talk. There was no let-up.

'Ye've nae thocht of takkin' silage? Ye hiv the pit …'

'I have the pit but the building's wrong. There's no way I could use a tractor at the back of the court. The passage is too narrow and the coos cannot reach the trough along there unless the court is brimful of muck! I can't stand that. Up to their bellies in muck!'

So pit silage was out and the rain hammered home Wullie's opinion about taking hay.

There was talk in the district about silage in a plastic tunnel, wrapped and stored in the field. Someone 'up north' had devised the technique for this process and a farmer who opted to try it out was well pleased with the result. A neighbour asked if John would like to go along with him to have a look first at the silage and then a bit further afield to see the machine doing its stuff. The idea was welcome. Anything was better than watching hay go dark as the rows flattened; a godsend also to Charlotte who was tired of pretending to be cheerful when she came in from looking at cows huddled together, sodden and dispirited like everything and everybody else. It was settled that they would set off on 'the morn's morn'.

The first call was brief but worthwhile. Admitting he expected it to cost him a bonny penny, the farmer was delighted with the process and the result. It had been quick, efficient and the silage the best ever. For him, haymaking was out from now on. They looked at a bale kept as a sample and agreed about the quality. The tunnel stretched the length of the park, black-packed winter feed ready and waiting. No wonder the man had a smile on his face.

They refused the offer of a dram and got underway for Banffshire. It was a change for John to ride in a car, without the thump of a diesel engine. Swiftly past the strange rusting sculptures at Lumsden, focus of many pawky jokes. Through Rhynie, Gartly and Huntly and on towards the coast. Neat farms, spoiled hay in many parks, small houses with the ubiquitous dormer windows and finally their destination.

Sandwiches and a cup of tea in a cheerful kitchen and then to business. The machine was at work in a nearby park and a lot was going on. They watched as a constant supply of bales was brought to the machine, wrapped and pushed tight into the final wrap of a tunnel. The farmer told them the

price of the machine and also the likely charge for a day's contracting within a reasonable distance. They managed not to look dismayed. Back in the Volvo, they agreed the whole thing was impressive. Neither was a wordy man and the miles rolled by with a great deal of thought going on. Bill spoke at last:

'Ye ken, John, It wid cost a fair bittie mair ...'

'A helluva lot,'

'But ... worth it?'

'In the long run ...'

More miles on the clock, Traffic slower through Huntly.

'I can see the banker's face but if I managed to buy ... my lads and me doing the hale thing, what d'ye think? Would you be likely ...?'

'I would.'

It was settled for the following year: Bill and his sons in the business of contracting for tunnelled silage with John as their first customer.

When that time came after a spell of nice weather likely to have raised thoughts of haymaking, the grass was cut and wilted and quickly baled. Over the brig trundled the vital tunneller and three very large tractors, all manoeuvred into a park close to the steading. Soon away to the farthest fields, two tractors picked up three bales on each trip, one lifted on a rear buckrake, two impaled by a wide front loader. All bales were put down alongside a third tractor placed next to the main machine. The third tractor's power loader lifted each bale and placed it on the long platform of the tunneller to be covered in plastic sheeting as it was pushed slowly along until tightly pressed against the bale wrapped previously. The tractor backed away leaving the bale double wrapped and in a further layer of plastic, i.e. tunnelled or tubed.

Watertight and airtight, with all the freshness of the silage preserved, a long, black tube snaked along the edge of the field. With plastic neatly tucked in and a straw bale rammed

at its end the tunnel was effectively sealed. Another tunnel was necessary to cover the quantity of bales taken. John had worked the near field, his John Deere tractor not man enough for three bales but the procedure the same, backing first to get a bale on the buckrake then forward to dig into a second bale, all in one neat movement. Speed was vital: bales had to come thick and fast to be wrapped. The need for several tractors resulted in high costs but John paid up, if not happily, weighing this against the many hours needed to recoup spoiled hay not to mention the slough of despond they found themselves in when rained off. The main advantage was the quality of the feed for the cows: he really hated feeding them indifferent stuff. When justifying the expensive tubes he made use of the cliché, 'You can't take it with you', but was unsurprised by an answer, 'If A canna tak' it A'm nae gaan!'

16

I Grow Old, I Grow Old

It has to be remembered that John and Charlotte were not in the first flush of youth when they made a move to become farmers. And now it seemed that time was slipping beneath the feet at a rate of knots. Charlotte was most aware: 'My hair! Beyond dyeing even if I could afford it.'

'No! It's just lighter, with the sun.'

It was late autumn, with a heavy sky over Bithnie Hill and a sharp wind tugging at leaves on the path: cows were lingering in the steading, one of the pointers that winter was in the offing with all it promised of gales, frost and snow. Cauldrife winter … Thoughts came into Charlotte's head from a casual conversation earlier in the day. She had been in the post office and someone was chatting at the counter. Another woman mentioned the cold and shaking her head over the summer gone by had touched on what might be in store.

'Ye'll ken noo aboot the snaa. An ye feel the coorse wither mair as ye git auld …'

Charlotte's airmail letter was weighed and needed more postage. Somehow no longer middle-aged she let the door slam behind her. She resolved to discuss the future and what they would do when the time came to retire: up to now it had not been on the agenda, they were too busy to think. It was difficult to imagine any sort of life without cows to look after or all the other farm work. And yet … John had been having

trouble with his knee – stepping from a tractor was hard on that joint – and the summer had been awful for the second year running. She wondered what John would have to say – probably not much.

Eventually, after a little delicate prompting, John did discuss the future. There was too much to do getting the farm up to snuff to even think of retirement but yes, he supposed the time would come. He promised to give it thought. Charlotte was fairly satisfied: like a Yorkshire terrier with its teeth into something he would consider every angle. She was from Yorkshire too and her brain was ticking over ...

Her first idea was to reduce the size of the herd and therefore the amount of work. Letting any surplus land would bring in regular income. But foreign bodies on their patch! She was pretty certain John would not agree, he liked the herd to be free from contact with other beasts and really she felt the same. In any case, fewer animals meant less income but not all that much less work.

What about getting someone in to help? A local man coming in daily or even living in the cottar house? A farm manager was quite out of their league, but someone to share the work? Yet who would want the job nowadays when every young person had the idea of getting famous by strumming a guitar or working in the 'media'. There was no fame to be had 'amang the muck'. She knew she was being unfair to all young things but did not expect one to apply or anyone older turning up out of the blue; a pensioner would not cope. John set a high standard and would be more harassed than ever if the help was not up to snuff. The seeds of disaster were there. She remembered someone whose man was always drunk ...

Selling half the farm and the old steading and putting up a small Atcost concrete building for their own animals on their half? Not on because of cost as well as the foreign neighbours, and too much trouble to sort out in any case.

They would have to think of something else or go on working for ever and ever.

Looking at the cottar house one day John said, 'Have you thought we could alter that for ourselves, make it really comfortable, with all mod cons and let the rest of the farm off to somebody like Gilbert? Someone you really liked and trusted to look after things well, working the way we do or even better since you are sure we are on this downward slope towards the knacker man?'

That was left hanging like the sword of Damocles, the implications unexamined. The reasons for and against cutting down, leasing, permanent help, selling land were left also, yet like a moth in a softly lit room is seen against the television screen but cannot be dealt with, they flitted in and out of mind, unresolved, spoiling the moment.

The pessimistic lady was entirely right. The weather worsened with the strong winds soon developing gale force and making life difficult. The *Oxford English Dictionary*, the shorter one, defines a gale as 'a wind of considerable strength'; in pop. lit. use 'a wind not tempestuous but stronger than a breeze'; in naut. use 'what on shore is called a storm'. The worst gale John experienced at sea was of force 12, hurricane force. A report which later proved false of a German invasion of the south coast of England had given cause for them, as the emergency destroyer, to make an urgent dash from Scapa Flow to Plymouth. They left Scapa in winds of storm force which turned to hurricane force, and suffered such damage that *Maori* was in serious danger. Guard rails and davits made of steel were twisted like barleysugar, the whaler was swept away and other boats crippled. Everything violently awash; messdecks deep in water with hammocks and all possessions floating about. A call from the skipper – 'CLEAR THE BRIDGE!' – the ship well over the known capsizing angle. Tossed and buffeted, a cork in a roaring maelstrom, somehow they reached

Londonderry and harbour. No member of the ship's company could place a foot onshore, but it was respite.

To Charlotte, 'considerable strength' and 'not tempestuous' lacked import, understated what could and did happen at Burnside and Bithnie when the stormwinds took hold. The Bible's 'rushing mighty wind' was nearer the mark and also 'filled all the house where they were sitting'. But even that could not convey the fearful scourging of the earth, the moaning obliteration of normality. Where iron sheets have gone weightless away, roofs gape and clatter the threat of worse despoil. All things not solid fixed are rolling, bouncing, curveting; they dip and are off again. Ownership and boundary are lost. Nowhere is there quiet.

The doors of the old steading at Bithnie were about 15 feet high and moved by wheels sliding along a steel track at the top. Unfortunately the doors were likely to jerk out of a small iron bracket meant to hold them at the bottom, and there was no track in the concreted floor. In any sort of through draught there would be movement: freed from the bracket the doors would bump and rattle, but in gale force winds the result was truly alarming. Wide heavy doors gusted almost at right angles to the building, banging down to lift again. Tremendous strain at the top with the threat of bursting out from the steel track and nothing to be done except wait for a lull and with little hope of success try to anchor them. Like the *Maori* surviving when over the capsizing angle, the outflung Bithnie doors never suffered the total destruction visualised but the sight of them at a fearful angle to the building was not forgotten.

It was after winds from hell subsided giving the Bithnie folks time to breathe and think again that John had the chance to go with Gilbert to an important show and sale at Perth. Assured by Charlotte that she had little to do except look at the cows, take a rest from cooking and maybe write a few letters, John was away. For once, there was nothing to

prevent him having the day off. The journey was reasonably easy though the whole of Scotland seemed to be heading for the event. First, a large breakfast to fortify them and the rest was bliss.

John was very quiet on his return to the farm. After an uneventful day Charlotte was ready to hear about the trip. She served supper, poured out a comforting dram and waited. It was only after the meal was cleared, the glass empty and both walked over to see their peaceful beasts settled for the night that confession came.

The Bithnie cows were to have company – John had bought seven more with calves at foot ...

17

They Say ...

Charlotte knew John would repeat the old chestnut all farmers used to justify spending money on livestock. In the Howe the spik went 'plan as if ye widnae see the morn's morn bit on-cairry as if ye wid nivver dee'. She remembered John Fowler telling them that when first they met, eyes twinkling in his nice face – he and his wife had been wonderfully helpful. However, seven cows with calves at foot, when the idea was to take things a bit easier, paving the way to retirement? To say she was surprised was understatement; flabbergasted was the word. Relief and was it triumph in John's expression made her want to hit him. She knew what he was going to say, his voice taking on a rather softer tone, like the one he used for the cows ...

'Wait. Don't fly off the handle, just wait till you see them.' What else could be done, except make her exit something of a flounce?

The newcomers were to arrive about lunchtime. John got ready for them and did most of the usual chores. Charlotte took time preparing a meal to eat earlier than usual and considered the situation, wishing she had found out more about cows good enough to tempt John. She trusted his judgement but was still annoyed, he had taken it for granted she wouldn't mind. To spoil truce came the memory of a previous delivery that went disastrously wrong.

A farmer they knew retired and John went to his roup and bought some animals. After a long and weary wait for them to arrive, a float tric-tracked over the bridge and made a slow way up the farm road. The driver's wife was also in the cab and clinging round her neck was a small baby. The diary recorded what happened:

FOUL weather. WIND/SLEET/HAIL.
Day of days – now and again you get 'em. Anxious about animals in such adverse conditions but unable to do much except bring the Highland twins into shelter. J there until 7 p.m. absolutely frozen stiff but stuck it out to get five cows and four calves. Their arrival at about 7.30 was a COCKUP (*sic*). Harry's son does not handle the float well and in addition he scurries down the ramp with a cow in pursuit – he had let out a calf belonging to a cow for Braeside penned in with ours. It was then the task to get Charley's animals back before ours could come out. The calf in the steading running along the corridor threatening to jump over into the court then kicked with both back legs into John's tum! Cow got into float without calf and then burst out again breaking the wooden float barrier and knocking John flying off ramp full length onto concrete. Tempers high. Eventually both back inside but float door would not shut. What relief to see him down the road. Have to calm our new cows totally upset by stramash over somebody else's animals.

And later:

NOT FINISHED YET. Phone calls. Confusion over nos 5 & 6. We have a calf too many! *Que dia*!'

Of course it got straightened out, things always did, but as Wullie remarked at the time, 'Yon lad made a richt bummle o' it!'

When the Perth cows came Charlotte wrote only: 'All ready. Specially strawed out and good hay and nuts for them. They are exhausted after the long journey,' but there was more to add because the next morning at 5 a.m. they awoke to sounds of distress – one of the cows was frantic and one of the calves was forlorn. No polite words for it. It was another COCKUP!

The eartags were checked and two did not tally. On the telephone to the haulier John at first got nowhere. Mr S about to leave for the Highland Show made a clever attempt to slide from under. After a little forcible persuasion he agreed to act. More delay because another farmer also intending to go to the Show now had to check his cows first. His call revealed that he was unsure but would drive to Bithnie to have a look. On sight of the bawling animal he said 'That's my heifer and I paid over £900 for her!' Accepting that he was right there must be a cow from him to match the orphan. John went back with him and luckily recognised one of the cows, BINGO – mother and child together and the man away with his lot and eventually to Edinburgh. Haulier now with a blot on his copybook.

Watching the mother giving the calf a good spit and polish John said, 'Good job he was fairly local. What if the cow had been mixed up with some off to the Orkneys!'

'You'll be saying "All's well that ends well" any minute now!'

18

Approved

Taking time to look at the new cows Charlotte admitted that they fitted the pattern of the herd. They were big and healthy-looking, had that sheen about them. She conceded that John had chosen well and accepted the situation, a *fait accompli* was not worth quibbling over. After the trauma of the float and the upset over the lost calf all had become calm. A distraction came with an unexpected telephone call from old friends. Alan and Lily were in Scotland, could they visit? It was a pleasure to see them. Of all people Alan and his family perhaps without realising it had most influenced their decision to farm. Something about their way of life, the independence and dedication of it had appealed strongly and the thinking began. Alan's reaction to Bithnie was most important because of that. Showing the whole farm up and down the braes, along rough tracks to the high point on Bithnie Hill to take in the wide spread of the Howe had to be rapid. Giving a bone-shaking and hilarious ride the Land Rover covered the ground. Parks and woodland, the river and the grazing animals were seen in rather fitful sunshine before any serious discussion but Alan pointed out to Lily the good stock and well-fenced parks. His verdict was wholehearted and generous, he was impressed by what they had achieved.

Lily had particularly enjoyed watching newly-hatched

67

goslings stumbling about in the back garden though Grey Gander was unwilling to allow her a close look. He tolerated Charlotte as the source of extra treats, bits of apple, handfuls of corn stolen from the cows and good thick slices of bread when he knocked at the door on behalf of his dames. She knew the way to divert his predatory yellow beak with a hand at his neck hardly ruffling the soft feathers but gently pushing him aside.

'While the goslings are so new almost all their water has to be drained away,' she told Lily. 'They're so drawn to water, absolutely determined to get into it but in seconds get waterlogged and could drown. The geese miss splashing about but do their best with the bucket.'

'I love the babies but have reservations about Papa.'

She was not mistaken about the look in Grey Gander's eye when in strange company.

When the delicate subject of the Perth sale came up Alan offered something from his own experience: 'Keep a little in hand rather than overstock – it leads to trouble. If your land supports X number always go below that.'

Shortly after the guests drove away there was a downpour of rain too late to spoil the visit but causing worry about the new calves. After a while Charlotte could bear it no longer.

'Let's bring them in, it isn't worth the risk …'

So into the steading trooped the lucky Perth cows and calves, while those already on the strength huddled under bordering trees waiting patiently for blue skies and gleams of sun: it is an unequal world for cows also.

The new calves were from a Belgian Blue bull. That breed was becoming popular and it was going to be interesting to see how they made out. Meantime in the steading with fresh hay and deep straw the calves soon became playful, frisking and tumbling about. With black splodges on white there was a strong resemblance to young Dalmations. The mothers rested and watched, cudding and content.

In the following days the diary had a brief entry: 'November weather continues – rain pours down and the mist lifts only temporarily'.

John tried and failed to separate the bull from the main herd to put him with the Perth seven but he was not having any, doubling back each time he was anywhere near the gate. This gave rise to the idea that one of the cows must be coming on heat; if he was moved he would miss that. There was no sign of oestrus from the new cows but it was time for them to be with the bull. Taken to the brae next to the herd, the usual exchange of noises followed, some could have been friendly and others not. After a while, opening the gate between them provided amalgamation and something of a romp. Pushing, shoving and bumping, clashing of heads and desultory fighting decided the order of the bunt and things settled down. The new calves stood out from the rest: they were one more step away from the old Angus breed.

Looking with some satisfaction at a peaceful herd, John justified buying the seven cows.

'Buying them wasn't against what Alan said. I've plenty of grass …'

But the words of caution from Alan had taken deep root in Charlotte's mind: 'What he said will "lie on my heart" like Mary Tudor and Calais!'

19

Throu-han

So after the Perth cows and their spotted progeny life at
Bithnie went on in the same way as season followed season,
giving weather of all kinds to enjoy or endure. Occasionally
they experienced hailstones in June and a sun warming
January would fail to gild a summer sky. An unrelenting
pressure of work allowed no relief to tired bodies and
sometimes the spirit flagged when tragedies inherent to
farming life called for stoicism. Countering all this was the
'sufficient beauty' of nature, the wide sweep of the land, the
many faces of the river and the mysteries of the wood. Black
tunnels of silage snaked across the paddock and good
harvests assured that the animals were well provided for.
There was pride in good stock and the nurture of their young
and cause to count these blessings.

It was a common dictum among the Scottish farmers that
if animals were failing or reaching the end of the natural
span of life it was better to 'send 'em doon the road' while
they were able to walk. Their favourite vet gave a wry
illustration of an opposite view by telling them of an old
farmer he met in his early days as an assistant in a semi-rural
practice. Reluctant to spend his bawbees on calling the vet to
a sick animal this man often left it too late, so the poor
creature was at the last gasp. Time after time this happened
causing the young vet to lose patience and give the man a

piece of his mind, detailing the many failures and consequent loss of income. When next the farmer called for assistance for another animal probably beyond help he specified: 'Dinnae send the laddie!'

It was impossible to ignore that the time was approaching when John and Charlotte should take the walk 'doon the road' leaving all joys and sorrows to some other farmer. They feared Bithnie might become part of a large concern with no one resident, a peripatetic workforce taking care of everything and both houses sold to defray some of the initial costs. Worse still was the prospect of cottage and farmhouse neglected and ending as heaps of stones. The buying up of family farms was a growing trend as they became less viable economically, the stuff of nightmares for the man with only a few acres. John and Charlotte tried to think of alternatives to retirement and found none – it seemed you either had to farm at full blast or give it up, acknowledging with regret that it was time to move on because your knees were getting 'jist a wee bit shooglie'.

The first sign that retirement had surfaced in John's mind came when both were in Aberdeen shopping for supplies and he seemed particularly keen on going home by way of King Street where he drew up outside a car showroom. Opening Charlotte's door he said a little too quickly,

'Come on, just for a minute, I want to show you ...' Standing in a premier place was a cream-coloured four-by-four vehicle from the Mercedes-Benz stable, very square and very sturdy. Charlotte looked, and then at John who had the blissful face that only something classic might evoke. His voice had emotion.

'What do you think? Would you like it?'

Charlotte had no understanding. 'Would I like it? Whatever for? We have the Land Rover.'

She caught sight of the price tag and looked at John. '*Madre de Dios*!' And more weakly in a pale version of the tennis player, 'You cainn't be serious?'

71

But he was. It was to be a 'retirement' vehicle. That was confirmed on a visit to Burnside to see John and Margaret and tell them what was in prospect. As always it was a pleasure to make this visit to congenial people in a familiar and dear place circled by hills almost blue in colour with Lochnagar gleaming in the distance. After the greetings there was admiration from John W., something of a connoisseur of cars.

'That is a retirement vehicle,' he said, 'if ever I saw one!'

Again the idea of selling the farm but retaining the cottage for themselves was considered. The view from there of the Howe in panorama was quite magnificent. In winter the little house tucked into the shelter of Bithnie Hill would have its comforts. It seemed worth going to the expense of an architect's vision of what could be done. His ideas were for the main room to have an inglenook fireplace and a polished oak floor; the kitchen extended to serve also as a dining room to have beautiful Italian tiles and all the latest equipment. There was little to be done about the bedrooms but the bathroom would be altered by designer pieces and a rolltop bath, plus more beautiful Italian ceramics completing the picture. Naturally this transformation of the Cinderella cottage was to cost a bonny penny. It was tempting, the vision of a room lined with books, with the big table and old Windsor chairs, pictures, the two of them disposed on sofas reading or listening to music in the glow of a huge fire in the inglenook. If by any chance they drank too much of wine or the water of life, the bathroom was there with its designer pieces and wonderful tiles ...

But it was not going to happen. Something fundamental had to be faced, an honest self-appraisal was necessary. With the best outcome of all – the farm bought by someone who lived in the farmhouse and whose animals would occupy the steading and the parks, what about the two lotus eaters from the smart cottage? As they strolled about in clothes

72

untouched by sharn or even a smidgeon of muck, a superior washer-dryer having dealt with that sort of thing, how would the new owner feel? In addition and more seriously, what if an animal was in trouble? Or neglected? Charlotte seeing a sign of mastitis and unable to act, John anxious about calving or unhappy about the care of a bull. Apart from whether spending a lot of money on what was a fairly basic cottar house was sensible, it came back to the tennis player: remaining at Bithnie as mere spectators would be 'the pits'.

20

On-gaan

John telephoned the architect and said nice things about his plans before delivering the chop. The account arrived next day, much more than expected but what else to do except pay it? Exploring options for life away from the farm was going to cost money but making the wrong move was sure to be more expensive in the long run. They took a look round the farm buildings trying to see what to retain and what to sell in the traditional farm 'roup'. A new owner might buy machinery, but should they consider selling 'lock, stock and barrel'?

This tour of the buildings generated shock. Bench with vice attached; fixed apparatus for bruising and sacking corn; tractors and implements to attach to them; carts, ploughs, turners, harrows, rotovator, scarifier, concrete-mixer; an elevator for bales; a power washer, a strimmer, picks, shovels, graips, rakes, mallets, hoes, scythes, forks, buckets, skeps, baskets, ropes. A great many tools.

'Where has it all come from?'

'That's only the tip of the iceberg!' John picked up a brass ventilator from a crate by the wall. 'This is from *Sargon* and over there things from *Banchu*, remember?' She did remember, the boats they had sailed, loved, and ventured in, Paris in springtime and *Banchu* moored within sight of the Pont Alexandre. Restaurant food superb but too dear so they

had eaten tinned food, mainly corned beef from their store in the bilges, but it had not mattered. And now this accumulation and treasure trove in boxes of spare parts, coils of wire, pieces of wood, this and that ...

'What about digging a deep hole?'

'Behind the cottage? Dump it?'

In their first year on Bithnie they had found the debris of years behind the cottar house and with difficulty cleared it, an effort almost forgotten as time slipped away like the waters of the Don beneath Bithnie brig.

Charlotte took responsibility for things in the house, resolving to do a little each day to get ready. Dealing with furniture and everyday things was no worry, what loomed larger in her mind was the store halfway between floors. Here when the Greys moved in they found a dartboard, a few tattered books and stray pieces of jigsaw puzzle, indicating use as a playroom. Light from a Velux window, good floorboards, a seat built along one wall, if repainted, carpeted and furnished, an obvious den or snug, a 'room of one's own' for someone. Transformation did not happen: things they had no time to unpack were left there and afterwards the place was useful for anything not thrown away because it might come in handy one fine day. The boat fittings, including the brass ventilator from *Sargon* had come into that category and sad to say so did empty cardboard boxes piled high. The fact that only rarely is there need for a good strong cardboard box does not inhibit the practice of keeping a good many of them safe.

Where to begin? Charlotte found herself moving things from one place to another, desultory inspection yielded nothing until the inevitable happened with a packet of letters, a photograph album ... the hour allotted to make a start on the big clearance passed without result except a reminder of how young they looked, John so smart in uniform and herself pencil slim in a flowery dress. How

different the world then: you hoped to survive but the thought of owning a house seemed absurd when all around were buildings reduced to rubble, whole areas flattened, streets with gaping holes where people once made a home, reared a family. To plan was almost to tempt providence: life was on hold until after the war.

The album set aside, wartime memories persisted as she prepared supper. John serving on destroyers in northern waters, in danger from the air, from submarine activity, from the sea itself. She had been in York when it was bombed and afterwards in Plymouth where once a tiny boy laughed comparing the whistling bombs and the nearness of an explosion saying, 'That was a good'un Sharl!' You had to hope there would not be another war, though evil people have power in a troubled world.

She mentioned finding the photographs and her surprise. 'I had forgotten ...' He began to sing, 'One day when we were young, remember that morning in May, you told me ...'

'Get your supper before it gets cold.'

He sampled the casserole of Aberdeen Angus beef and dumplings light as air. 'Somehow or other that young sylph learned to cook ...'

21

A Proper Snorl

Two hours to spare. With some regret Charlotte climbed the stairs. There were so many things to be done, housework, farm accounts, VAT or in protest she might have picked up *Barchester Towers* and had the treat of Archdeacon Grantly and Mr Slope, but the store must be cleared and she had made up her mind to be ruthless. Moving everything from the green-painted seat made the floor more crowded but there had to be space for the separate piles, things to keep, to throw away or to give, this charity pile likely to be meagre. She tore the first from a roll of bin-bags and opened it ready for loot.

A boxful of clothing yielded Helly-Hanson thermals, shrunken and worn but kept in case of major climate change, a new Ice Age? Stuffing them into the bag gave the glow of being ruthless and yet it might be wiser ... she decided to have an extra pile, for things to throw away later when you were absolutely certain, with the removal van at the door, so to speak. She opened another bag for throw-outs and pushed into it a 1960s overcoat, made by a Prime Minister's great friend. Lord Kagan had had his day and Harold Wilson resurgent was not the style to inflict on student or layabout or even on a combination of the two. A 13-inch television of early date was patently rubbish. Renewed glow at one bag filled and one emptied box. A brass jelly pan that could or

should be polished and sold but how many people made jam nowadays? From Craigie Step, a croft on Burnside land, ten children had marched to school with a 'Jeely piece' to eat for lunch. She could not forget that picture of the little tribe leaving the 'Teuchatshoose', the house of the lapwings.

There were quantities of clay pots to keep and some nice ones for house plants: having time to fill them would be strange. The keeping pile was growing. She decided against a quantity of polystyrene packing as even when you could have used it you never remembered where the stuff was. Better to ditch now. There had to be doubts about boxes of glasses, people gave you things like that and sometimes they were free samples. Would the charity shop want them or the discarded spectacles at one time collected, did they still do that, send them overseas to help unfortunate eyes? Very old binoculars followed whisky tots and old specs into the undecided bag. Alarm clocks never again to rouse a sleeper were tossed onto the polystyrene, followed by one wellington boot.

The holdall containing souvenirs of John's trip to the oil rig offered no problem. The keeping pile was much the largest. China ornaments, Beswick-ware cows and bulls and a pig painted prettily with roses, a frivolous buy. Then catching at the heart, her father's old wallet, its beneficences long gone, as he was.

Progress slowed at the next box. Account books, invoices, how long did you have to keep these? Perhaps some could go but it was not the time to decide. No pencil to make a note, so she would have to remember ... To her dismay the next box yielded files, so many she would need more space, perhaps on the big table downstairs, but a decision about them would have to be later. Then a box of John's: he could see to that; she would throw away the wrong things if she tackled it. The 'later' pile was mounting.

From a swathe of tissue paper she took a pewter jug with a copper lid, a pleasant thing kept on a windowsill in the old

house. How many times she had stopped dusting to look at the garden and blossoming trees: sometimes geese had been on the pond, rippling the water in an elegant glide so different from their ambling walk. Memories came to a halt when a shout came from below:

'Can you come? Bit of a stramash!'

It took seconds only to get to the door, into wellingtons and across to the steading. One of the things about farming was the sudden crisis, a call to 'action stations' as at sea.

It was a fight. A real humdinger of a head to head between two Angus cows so similar that it was impossible to name them even when they parted to draw breath. No quarter was asked or given, the crack of bone on bone, the grunting, groaning clash was horrible to see and hear. Worse still when Charlotte realised that one 'fechter' was a newly-calved cow, and hardly steady on its feet, the new calf was dangerously close to the battle. Fortunately not all the herd was there.

'I need to get her out, with the calf. First the calf ...' Easier said than done. Piteous in a strange new world it dodged away among the watching bodies; the court not yet strawed out was lumpy underfoot. The chase disturbed spectator cows, some moved uneasily, bolder ones became frisky, gambolling about the court. Still fighting, the mother was aware of manoeuvres towards the gate and when they got the calf out, was desperate to follow. It was essential to avoid the fight moving onto concrete outside the court, but as luck would have it the wrong cow reached the gate and lurched towards the calf. Anguish from mother left inside. It took time to sort out.

'How on earth?'

John explained: 'They were both on the point, and Zelda calved first. Zoe immediately claimed the calf ...'

'I wouldn't think fighting the best preparation for her, when she manages it.'

They had Zelda and the calf isolated but cosy in a turnip

shed. Zoe had gone snorting off up the brae and John intended to follow. 'I'll come too.' Charlotte was anxious and not hopeful of a trouble-free birth.

'No. Get the supper and with a bit of luck I'll be back. Remember what Gilbert told us?'

'Some of them calve just like shelling peas!'

It was hard to believe in a shelled pea for Zoe.

22

An Mair

John found Zoe at the top of the brae, well screened by a patch of whins. He saw blood on her but in the failing light could not tell if there was a calf. Becoming aware of him, in the cussed way of calving cows she decided to move off along the brae, the walk purposeful as if she had another refuge in mind. After making sure no calf was hidden away, John followed. She stood for a time beside a crumbling dyke and then took the same purposeful walk down the brae, along the path and back to the steading. There he found her eating hay with obvious relish. She met his eye in an unflinching stare: a bonny 'fechter' like Zoe can ignore a bit of language.

John felt better after supper and ready for Zoe. She was going to calve, the question was when. She moved off and John followed but this time more easily in a tractor. She took a different direction and stopped at the stream near the farm's eastern boundary, nosing under the spread of junipers there, then drank before turning back. He kept very still: he guessed she was aiming for a sheep fold protected by strong walls and bordered by silver birch trees. He was right. She crossed the stream and disappeared into shelter.

It was not too comfortable in the *Zetor* but John had everything he needed including a flask of coffee. There had been many vigils of this kind and always time took on a slower beat as if in awe of what might come. Small sounds from

flowing water touched a silence brought by the darkling sky and all things waited …

When a glimmer of light broached the night John moved to peer over the dyke, taking care not to disturb or frighten the cow away from a perfect place for the birth. Half-light saw a beginning and all the normal stages followed. She got to her feet kicking at the belly, wandered about, going down again, getting up … frequent pains, her breath strained and fast … then quiet before much fiercer pain and at last the sight of a water bag meant the head and forelimbs were being forced into the birth channel, the tips of the hooves approaching the vulva. Pink bladder out further and further to rupture in a rush of fluid, the hooves clear to see but not the nose. Help was needed.

John moved to her side; she would no longer care about escaping him. He put lubricant on his hands before grasping the legs to push the whole calf back to release its head caught at the top of the birth channel and stuck there. The firm downward pressure on the head should then get it into a normal position, ready for birth. John felt sure he had managed to correct the position of the calf but the cow remained an inert heap, matted, stained and bloody in the increasing light. It seemed a long time before there came a sudden violent expulsion of a calf, a big bull calf. Zoe lay there uncaring while John cleared mucous from its twitching jaws.

'A heifer would have been useful lassie but he'll do nicely!'

It was a relief that both were alive. He waited until the calf was on its feet and sucked. That first suck was the stuff of survival; colostrum had vitamins, antibodies and a little natural purgative.

John washed his hands and arms in the burn then as an afterthought dunked his head, gasping and spluttering at the arctic cold. It had a wonderful restorative effect. He climbed into the *Zetor* and trundled back. Into his mind there came a tantalizing vision of a bacon sandwich.

Debbie feeds Mole

Safe haven

Tommy

G-Wagen

A wee bit snaa

Tiger Muffin

The tubes

Good Bithnie
stock

Drinking with
a little bit of
help

Barron Hall
view from
patio

St. Monans
Church

Barron Hall

Charlotte checked on Zoe and the little bull and after a later visit suggested it might be wise to have them down in the steading – there was something about the calf that made her uneasy. Wullie had arrived on the farm and went with John to get the cow and calf. Zoe was strangely submissive and allowed them to shepherd her away from the fold, seeming not to care whether or not the calf would follow. Halfway to the steading the bull calf sank down and would not be prodded to his feet.

'Dinnae lift him John, ye'll dae yersel a mischief, he's a big bugger.' Wullie then picked up the calf and with giant strides was away down the brae. At the gate he stopped, seeing a wheelbarrow left outside the cartshed.

'A han-barra's jist the ticket!' he beamed and shovelled in his burden. Unfortunately not only was the calf galvanised into life and out of the barrow but Zoe took fright, reared and went galloping after him away up the brae back to the *querencia*, her birthing place. She did not share Wullie's opinion of the wheelbarrow.

With some sweat it was rectified.

'You trying to kill me, Wullie?'

'A'll tak a skeeg on the backside!'

Charlotte had the coffee ready.

'Will you put her in the crush John?'

'When she's rested. And me!'

'A'll gie ye a han.'

It was accomplished, Zoe wary but not in 'fechtin' mode Charlotte made a glucose drink and managed to get the calf to take some. Removing the bottle, John quickly steered the little bull alongside the cow, its head to the bag. Nosing everywhere except at the teats he found a mouthful of hair and sucked half-heartedly at that.

'Yon tits are awfu' thick!'

That was the trouble, the calf seemed to be repelled by what offered his best hope for survival. Clamping his jaws

round a teat failed time and again; he simply would not suck. Alarmed when the calf sank, head on one side, spluttering, John made the decision.

'Belay there!' He lifted the lever to release Zoe. He was pleased to see her move swiftly to the calf, licking and pushing at him, making concerned little noises. It seemed like bonding ... The two were guided to the Dutch barn where the cow could nibble at hay bales and getting them back for a second effort in the crush would be easy. The gander chuntered his displeasure as he moved his dames away, having no doubt at all whose barn it was.

The later attempt had an awkward start with Zoe unwilling to enter the crush but after a swallow of glucose the calf was coaxed onto a teat and sucked briefly. When he would not be persuaded to try again John called it a day. However little, he had something to sustain him, some milk had gone down. Also other animals had to be looked at before the long day ended.

Very early next morning what joy to find Zoe standing to suckle. For quite a time the little Angus worked at one teat and then moved on to another. The morning air was the sweeter for it ...

23

A Sicht For Sair Een

Nature triumphant for once. Witnessing Zoe and the calf on the way to solving their own difficulties was a bonus: usually sessions in the crush had to be repeated many times. Following periods of stress, once in a while came days which Charlotte called 'near-halcyon'. As a child she had loved hearing the story of Halcyone and remembered this later when John was in the Service. After her husband perished in a shipwreck, Halcyone in an agony of grief threw herself into the sea to drown. The gods in compassion changed the two of them into birds and decreed that when the female was breeding calm would prevail. Unfortunately John experienced no 'halcyon days' at sea but on the farm they did occur, perhaps not entirely calm but reasonably so, hence the qualification.

Crisis over and the sun shining, it really was a good day and for once there was time to spare.

'Could you possibly cut my hair?'

'Yip!'

An old sheet to wrap him round and a pair of scissors, a rug rolled back and the serious attack on the growth of weeks, or even months, began. The short back and sides hair style for men was not *de rigueur* but there had to be some limit. Charlotte was pleased with the sharpness of the implement sending dark hair streaked with grey to fall at her

feet. 'I think I'm a natural snipper.' She stood back to admire the first inroads.

'Well, hurry up, Just take a bit off so it clears my collar.'

'No. No. I want to do it properly. Ship-shape and whatsit fashion!'

She started again, engrossed in the effort of balancing each side, it meant going back, taking more off here and there.

'Honestly, Charlotte, that's enough!'

She removed the sheet and went to get the dustpan and brush. John lacked patience. However, if he found the lopsidedness disturbing she might get another shot at it.

John went out to shake himself free of hairs and saw at the top of the farm road a car he did not recognise as a local car. Neither did he recognise the two people who got out and walked to the house, so at the door he was unprepared for the woman advancing with open arms, or the man smiling behind her. Both were well dressed: spruce, he thought, unlike their usual visitors. Must be for Charlotte. And yet … the woman kissed him warmly on both cheeks, and then again. Her perfume contrasted with what he feared was his farm smell. Had she gained a few of his stray hairs as well?

'My dear! We thought we'd never find you!'

'Come inside. Charlotte's here.'

She wasn't and he guessed she had chickened off to smarten up a bit. Women were like that.

When she appeared Charlotte had combed her hair and was tidier. She got kissed, perhaps with less gusto. The handshake was cordial.

'Coffee?' she asked, and busied herself with cups.

'Shall we go through?' The sitting room should be tidy; these friends of John's looked, well, a bit smart.

'Please, please, no fuss!' insisted the lady. 'So lovely, a farmhouse kitchen!' Something in the statement was suspect. Newspapers strewn about, odd clothes, tufts of hair

Charlotte had missed and worse if you looked hard enough – not *House & Garden* at all.

'Tell us all about yourselves!'

'If you have a couple of hours.' Offhand he sounded. Charlotte knew John needed to get back to work but she did not want to be left. And why did he not give her something of a clue? He had not introduced them, just mumbled something about old friends.

She listened to their impressions of Scotland, registering that they had stayed at Gleneagles for several nights and before that at Edinburgh's oldest and best hotel. It seemed they did not have to count the pennies. The woman's hair was a delicate ash blonde, her clothes were very nice. The husband was pleasant, well groomed. He seemed to listen with great affection when his wife talked – she looked at a manicured left hand. Yes, his wife. Charlotte asked them to stay to lunch but the visitors had to press on, were due elsewhere.

'Let me help you with these' said the man, scooping up his wife's cup and saucer, 'Camilla will be too busy talking to John about old times!' Charlotte's own cup dropped onto the draining board with a clatter. Camilla! That was Camilla!

Returning from the kitchen they found old times were not being discussed. Camilla was alone, gathering up gloves and a stylish handbag.

'John is getting us a map, darling.' She took her husband's arm and turned graciously towards Charlotte.

'And now we really must be off – so lovely to have seen you both, an absolute highlight!'

John came back to hand the map to 'darling' whose name was still a mystery as he edged the sleek car carefully down the farm road.

'God, I thought they'd never go and I'm anxious about Marigold. I'll get along there before we eat if you don't mind.'

'I don't mind in the least. Take your time.'

Years ago when she became engaged to John one or two people had mentioned Camilla, as if they had not liked her very much. One man had been gleeful – 'So you've rescued John from a fate worse than death!' Another explained, 'We feared Camilla would get him!' At that blissful moment she had taken little notice and John laughed saying, 'No chance!' Now and again the name cropped up, especially in later newspaper reports about a royal person, and John had put on a daft look, his hand to his heart and vowed, 'Ah Camilla! Not easy to resist a Camilla!' Now she had seen the old flame in the flesh. Or was she at their wedding? Charlotte could not remember.

'Marigold's OK.'

She served lunch and waited for him to speak but his question was unexpected.

'Come on, spill! Who was your boyfriend? I sat there like a Tom Tit waiting for you to tell me.'

'You sat there! I was waiting for you!'

To say John was flabbergasted when she broke the news would be an understatement.

A letter from Lisa shortly afterwards had a postcript:

We met Camilla and Gerald Bland in town and they mentioned visiting you. Said the farm was very nice! And (Camilla) that John looked healthy but 'not the same'. What did she mean about his hair? Write when you can. Love …

'And you really and truly didn't recognise her? She looked … I don't know, expensive? … high maintenance.'

John had recovered himself. 'I really and truly didn't recognise Camilla but thought it odd my heart beating so fast and then this overwhelming sense of loss. Nearly fell over Marigold! I need TLC.'

'You'll get a skeeg!' Wullie's vocabulary was always a help.

24

Seen as Red

Marigold calved. As usual with the breed she did it by herself, was unwilling to be watched or helped. Shaggy long hair, red-gold in the sunshine, Highland cows are beautiful to look at as they graze. A local hotelier kept three or four because his guests liked to see them. No wonder the Scottish artists Peter Graham, William Watson and Henry Garland loved them and painted the cattle standing by water, drinking or gazing into the distance while around them the mountain slopes are shrouded in mist. From the genes of ancestors reared on such terrain the Highland has retained an independent character which on Bithnie often led to trouble. John and Charlotte were very serious about the ownership of animals: if you took on this responsibility there were no half measures, your best effort was needed. Food, shelter and watchful care were fundamental and if as a result of treating your stock well you gained their trust it made things easier in situations requiring them to be handled, or helped, as in calving. The most perfect example of this was dear old Lucy, long gone to graze in the Elysian Fields. With Marigold and company rapport did not happen; they could not manage to trust humankind.

The udder on a Highland cow is difficult to see: a new calf might suck at a mouthful of hair instead of the teat. If treatment was needed it could be one helluva job with

certain sweat if not tears involved. Threatening when a calf was on the way, likely to move off at speed if a watcher came too close, when the calf was born only a foolish farmer would rush to check the gender. All in all the little gang included in the Bithnie herd proved labour-intensive: their heifer calves were kept but no further Highlands were purchased.

Charlotte walked on the path at the top of the braes after having a look at Marigold. There was a quality in the light, a softness and stillness to the day and a bloom of flowers to make her reluctant to go inside the house, but the store was unfinished, a clearance had to be made if ever the farm had to be open to inspection, ready for a purchaser.

The place was a chessboard where boxes had been moved into new positions rather than banished. On the narrow green seat black bags loomed as spectators. Stale air, dust and a smell of old paper were intolerable on such a day and Charlotte was quick to adjust. Scooping up the box put on one side in a previous foray she took it into the kitchen and put the coffee pot on the Aga.

The files emptied onto the table were old and seemed strangely unfamiliar as if different people had collected them, amassed the contents in another life as remote from the present as it was possible to be. Charlotte's instinct was to discard them as of little importance yet she had to look. Were they kept for a reason or because there was never time to sort and discard, keep a minimum? Was this very day the moment of truth?

She opened exercise books labelled 'Ethics', 'Philosophy', 'Psychology'. It was interesting to see what young minds had been expected to assimilate: the notes made were neat and precise. A lecture room rose from memory, tiers of naive girls hardly enthralled by an old professor droning on in a foreign accent … herself trying hard, always the swot. However, scribbled on the cover of the philosophy notebook was an extract from Bernard Shaw's *Major Barbara*:

No capacity for business, no knowledge of law, no sympathy with art, no pretension to philosophy; only a simple knowledge of the secret that has puzzled all the philosophers, baffled all the lawyers, muddled all the men of business and ruined most of the artists; the secret of right and wrong. Why man, you're a genius, a master of masters, a god. At twenty-four too!

She would show John that before the notes went as waste-paper. And what about her essay on communism? He would enjoy that and suggest a Tory matron lurked there beneath the certainties. She had bought a copy of the *Communist Manifesto* to study, then somehow lost it. Horror of horrors, her name in large letters on the cover and there it was somewhere in the world labelling her as a red. It was so unfair and worried her at the time. She had written: 'The aim of the communists was to raise the proletariat to the position of ruling class. There is nothing distinctive about it except the shift of class power.'

That was not bad if you consider the trade unionists and politicians who are ennobled, the pop singers and foot-ballers, who are 'Sir This and That'. *Plus ça change…*

It was useless trying to go through the files. The fact was they were interesting, to her at least. Could be classified as the historical data of one Charlotte Elizabeth, farmer hoping to be a retired farmer if ever store, house, barns and all the rest were cleared up. She put the box on the stairs ready to carry up.

25

Voyages Closed and Done

The cattle took up much of the time but there was plenty to do without thinking of a sale. The box containing papers relevant to John had been left for him to deal with: Charlotte could not or would not see to it. When they moved to Bithnie they made a list and had worked steadily through it, first to rid the place of eyesores such as decrepit sheds, a railway carriage and several wrecked cars and then over a long time they renewed fences, gates, re-seeded all except the high braes and cleared much of the woodland. John was farm boss with limited authority elsewhere, Charlotte was farm slave, cook and boss of the house: the system worked very nicely. In the house a fireplace with a very small grate was replaced by one of local stone suitable for the massive log fires needed in winter. John took a lot of trouble to get that looking good and functioning properly. Eric, a tiler who had renewed floors in the Burnside house, was tracked down working for another firm and came to put quarry tiles in the old dairy, the kitchen, pantry and lobby. New carpets for the stairs, the hall and in a couple of rooms, but when they decided to have the same carpet for the remaining rooms they were told the design was no longer stocked. The period between being a prime choice and becoming obsolete was roughly 12 months. Though roses still flowered unfaded over bedroom walls, their impact was minimal, seen on waking or by very

tired eyes. All in all it could be said that the Bithnie folk had not spent much time 'loutherin aboot'.

Getting John to look at his box was not easy. He did not refuse to look, agreed often that it was necessary to sort the thing out, yet action did not follow. *Mañana* appeared to be the operative word. In an attempt to get the box cleared Charlotte carried it downstairs and spread out the contents on the kitchen table where John could not fail to see them. First out was something with both bulk and weight, a very battered English Channel handbook. Originating from the Hydrographic Department of the Admiralty the contents in the form of a loose file were dog-eared and spotted with damp, the faded cover near to collapse. The book was compiled for ready reference in small craft and originally charted an area from Ramsgate to the Scilly Isles on the English coast and from Dunkirk to Douarnenez on the French coast. John's edition had been enlarged to include the Thames Estuary and the Bristol Channel together with additional chartlets of small ports on the French coast. Charlotte could not resist riffling through the pages; vivid happenings came to mind … the approach to Le Havre and the Seine Estuary, *Banchu* so small and the great bulk of the *Isle de France* looming … what a time to arrive when that colossus was leaving and how uncomfortable her wake made them. To the *Bassin de Yachts* with in her case a deal of tension to release with the anchor. At sea when the waves were mountainous and the boat a crab crawling up, managing to breast them and then sliding down, down until the next one to climb, the traitorous thought would come – why oh why am I here? She would look at John and he would grin. It was not always better in a yacht basin, with an unhappy mix of wakes and incoming waves and tides, even John could feel sick and suggest going ashore.

John came in and seeing the book jumped to a conclusion. 'Oh, good, you're doing it …'

'Not on your life. It's your stuff.' The opened pages had the same effect, took him back to *Banchu*.

'My God, Southampton, Le Havre, the buoys marking the fishing worried me no end ... Do you remember?'

It was engrossing, reliving their first trip when underestimating the tide and rather mistiming their passage up the Seine they had been caught by the tidal bore, swept like a bobbing cork downstream ...

'Something of a cockup!'

Comical in retrospect but frightening then. They had managed to get alongside a massive barge, helped by willing hands. The master of the barge *Robert* had invited them aboard, given them wine and offered a tow all the way, *entente* most *cordiale*. Early next morning they were away and not long afterwards moored in Paris.

The European trips became routine, events, people, arose out of the past, differing a little in recall ... John had liked the adventurer who had brought his new wife across the Atlantic in a tiny amphibian jeep, their honeymoon trip! Charlotte thought him crazy and pitied the wife. They remembered the bonhomie of the well-off QC who bought *De Bries*, a Dutch barge formerly owned by filmstar Diana Dors ... and also young Englishmen from the home counties having a final fling before one of them got married.

'See you sometime,' a shout as they passed *Banchu*.

'Perhaps tomorrow!' Their boat was overflowing with local beauties ... a last shout in Franglais ... 'Perhaps nev ... airre!'

But all the reminiscing in the world did not deflect from the purpose: 'And now for the rest John, I'll leave you to it!' She was certain the English Channel handbook would be kept.

26

Redded

The black rubbish bags were disposed of and charity shops in Aberdeen were a little richer. Several boxes were neatly piled on the narrow seat and the floor was reasonably clear: Charlotte's mission to reduce baggage in the store was accomplished. That word was a favourite, pronounced as William Henry Vine, star of the church choir when she was young, in a thrilling tremolo had sung from the Messiah, (it was) ac-compli-shed.

The house would bear inspection. A prospective buyer could assess the general working of the farm, look at the land, farmhouse and empty cottar house. The contents of the buildings were another matter but did not hold up the big decision of who would handle a sale and when exactly was the best time to start things off. The Mart frequently dealt with selling farms but there were other agents with possibly wider access to the country as a whole. It was decided to approach a firm in Banchory and so it was they became acquainted with Ronald and eventually Sara, his assistant.

It might be said that Ronald looked the part in his country tweeds. An outdoor man with a ruddy complexion and easy manner, he could talk to farmers and was comfortable among cattle: his green wellies had seen mud. Before settling on the agency Charlotte had queried whether Bithnie was

quite in their league. Selling great estates with zillions of pounds at stake was their forte.

'Not to worry,' John had said: 'Someone has to pay the tea lady! Commission from us might just do that!'

So Ronald walked the land and talked the talk and they fixed a price and set in motion all the procedures to do with selling the farm. Photographs were taken of house and garden, of growing crops and grazing animals. A brochure can be a work of art and after a few corrections by an eagle-eyed if not pernickety Charlotte, they were pleased with Ronald's effort. The first page carried an excellent photograph taken from high on the brae and reaching to distant blue hills. Bithnie was described as 'situated in the delightful surroundings of Donside with extensive views over traditional farmland and hills ...' There was 'An extensive range of sporting facilities within easy reach, from skiing, golf and hill-walking to the more traditional pursuits of shooting and fishing on some of Scotland's most prestigious estates and rivers ...'

Reading this made John regret not spending time on some of the pursuits: truth to tell he was too often 'amang the muck'. One point was emphasised, that 'The farm, as a result of its boundaries, is located in such a way that no other farm immediately borders it. This has a considerable beneficial effect in that no animal or crop diseases are carried across boundaries and onto the farm and therefore the land is in an exceptionally clean condition ...' Charlotte had a comment: 'You prompted that John, it has your stamp all over it!'

'His words, my message. But he agreed it was massively important.'

Advertisements appeared in the national press and one in the *Press and Journal*, caused a good deal of speculation. Of course this 'spik' was relayed to John and Charlotte, the opinion of older farmers and one or two younger locals who inherited family farms and knew nothing of the rough and

tumble of the property market, that too high a price was asked. Years ago the same thing had been said about Burnside, becoming almost legendary, that John 'winted his heid examint paying such siller for a wee bit ferm!'. Since those kind words, time and the market had moved still further on.

Wullie helping John on the farm caught sight of Sara from Banchory: impressed, he could not resist the old joke: 'Ay John! Fin ye see sic bonny quines ye winner far aa the soor-faced aal wifies come frae!'

Though unused to a farm assignment Sara did her best and it was pleasant when the faultless accent fluted over the wires with an appointment to view. Ronald was truly the boss and driving force, managing the change from *haute monde* to family farm with some enjoyment.

And so the vague idea of retirement became reality. Somehow when arrangements were in process and decisions were taken and the house was in an unusual state of tidiness, the business of the farm went on. Animals were fed, cared for, treated for ills large and small, as normally. The annual test for brucellosis was once again endured and proved as exhausting as ever. Visitors came and went. Things that were of little import before the decision to sell became suddenly immediate. They had been so busy getting the farm up to snuff for someone to buy that one very important factor was not discussed. If they were successful and sold the farm they would have to leave, find somewhere else to live.

27

Fae aa the Airts an Pairts

A surprising attempt was made by another agent to horn in on the agreement made with Ronald's firm. There were telephone calls and a Sunday visit from a very keen young man who stressed that their selling commission was less by half a per cent, quite a considerable sum if you worked it out, but John had commissioned Ronald and that was that. 'Have you signed anything?' was the question John did not trouble to answer. Throughout the time the farm was for sale this nuisance of a man kept on, asked if he could produce a brochure with photographs, if he could introduce a possible customer. His blandishments were useless, the answer brief: 'Get in touch with Ronald!'

The weather turned nasty. Gales swept the farm and two corrugated sheets disappeared from the steading roof. Rain followed and heavy mists shrouded the hill. It was not good for viewing. However, two people from Wales who had sold a farm wanted to see Bithnie. The day of their arrival was slightly better and they did not get wet walking over the parks, were safely inside and drinking coffee before rain came. In conversation it emerged that their farm had been much smaller than Bithnie. Reinforcing an impression that money could be a sticking point, to Charlotte the wife expressed doubt that there would be enough to stock the larger acreage or indeed whether the two of them could

manage the extra workload. So it looked negative but not a waste of time as they were a serious young couple with the right ideas about animal welfare and might have been very suitable for Bithnie. After they had gone and John and Charlotte discussed the visit, coming to the same conclusion of 'Nice but unlikely', it was a surprise to hear from the agent that the two were very impressed, were considering an offer and had visited the banker to talk money. Shortly after this telephone call came another arranging for a second viewer from Wales. What was happening there, they wondered, why the population shift? The chance to ask did not come because the visit was cancelled: a later appointment was promised.

Meanwhile the steading roof gaped as a bad advertisement and here Charlotte took a stand. She conjured up a lurid picture of makeshift ladders not quite man enough to reach the high arch of the roof, their total collapse leaving John outlined on the concrete floor like a television corpse, surviving only to bid a weak farewell. A small victory when Mr Anderson of Clatt came and did the repair in three and a half hours. His ladders were adequate.

A cold spell of weather but plenty of sun for the arrival of the next people, Mr and Mrs Ellis, also from Wales.

'People are deserting their homeland in droves,' decided Charlotte, ever ready for drama. They were very young, the Ellises, the man slightly older than his wife who looked about 16 years old. They walked the farm but became separated, Mr E with John and his wife with Charlotte. When they left, full of excitement and promises, it was hard not to be amused.

'He told me his family history, they've been farmers and dealers since the year dot.'

'It's hard to believe but the girl told me their financial situation down to the last penny. How much in the bank, the total when their sale is completed and what is promised from parents! I felt embarrassed.'

'Maybe they've never been in a situation like this, buying or selling. Would you ever do that?'

'Never in a million years. I was taught never to discuss money or religion.'

'Religion and politics I thought!'

All in all they were not hopeful of a sale.

The Brothers Karamazov were next, not exactly their name but so much a pair that the nickname stuck. They could have been twins but it seemed impolite to ask. Both tall, sturdily built, with black hair and prominent white teeth ready to smile when the eyes did not. To say they were farmers was an understatement: they were farmers *par excellence*. During their patrol of the land not a fence or gate's fastening was untested, no blade of grass escaped scrutiny. The shortcomings of the old steading building were pointed out, machinery observed with a curl of the lip or lips, the market value of each animal registered in an almost audible click of each brain. Professional was the word for them. They left in cheerful fashion after a combined attempt to discover how much under the rumoured figure John was prepared to accept.

'God's teeth!' A release of breath from John. 'It was like being put through a wringer!'

'I didn't care for them. That hair and the smiles.'

She was puzzled, 'They were so much of a mind yet I sensed, what, competition between the two?'

'Maybe, but both would like to get Bithnie at a cut price.'

'Then who would have the house and who the cottage?'

It was impossible to visualise. The cottage modernised and extended might become superior to the farmhouse and give angst. Or if one brother lived on the farm and the other had a daily journey would the traveller be tempted to buy himself a superior car or even a Mercedes G-Wagen? It did not take much to set off wilder speculation. Such was the aftermath left by the Brothers Karamazov. Charlotte did not change her opinion and did not want them to buy the farm.

100

It seemed that people from Wales liked the look of Bithnie because both families intimated that they would like to put in an offer as required by the Scottish system of buying property. Like the Greys when first looking to buy a Scottish farm, they found that system strange with no fixed price stated but offers requested by a specific time. What to bid? A fair offer might be somewhere between what could be afforded and what the owner expected and a wide range of bidding could result: an inspired guess was needed. However, somehow or other property was bought and sold.

With regard to Bithnie, the first couple were trying to juggle their finances and the second had disclosed theirs to Charlotte via the young wife.

Another viewer was a man who long ago had told John he had been 'pipped at the post' by their bid for Bithnie. He seemed impressed by the improvements made since those early days but he too was nearing retirement and his interest concerned his sons. One of the problems of the old-style farmer was that his land could not now generate sufficient income for more than one family, so the most dedicated young son often had to seek work elsewhere. There was also a greater degree of expectation from the young men; they did not fancy scraping a meagre living when the world beckoned with more exciting promises. Even the more prosperous landowners faced this dilemma: John had encountered it long ago when he bought his first pure Aberdeen Angus cow. A well-known breeder had confessed that his sons were not interested in what had been his life's work and pleasure, they were too highly educated to become 'fermers'.

People came who were not sent by Ronald but by the thrusting young man avid for commission on the sale of Bithnie. John was looking among the Angus cows for a calf he had treated with antiseptic powder for cuts on its face, the check necessary in case the little bull and his mother had to be brought down to the steading for more thorough

treatment. The calf was in his sights when also into view came two people emerging from the nearby wood. John walked towards them.

'Good morning. May I ask who you are and how you happen to be on my land?'

He gave them what Charlotte described as 'one of his looks', perhaps a relic from service life it was a straight-browed concentrated gaze that could be intimidating.

The man gave an easy laugh. 'There's no law of trespass in Scotland is there?'

He was well dressed and confident: His companion waited, looking into the distance as if she found the encounter vastly boring.

'So your purpose is …?'

Again the easy response. 'I understand this farm is for sale and we're taking a look around! I must say the cattle look well. How many head …'

He was interrupted: 'Viewing this farm is done by appointment only and I know you have no appointment. If you care to make one with my agent …' He moved off to find the calf.

Surprisingly an appointment was made through Ronald but only after a telephone call from the would-be agent answered by Charlotte. He had sent the people to have a look round: they were very 'well-off'. His voice took on a wheedling note – he knew John was a first-rate chap but could he be more 'neighbourly'. She might 'give a little whisper'. She was both irritated and amused. Whisper in John's ear? 'Dear one, please go around spreading sweetness and light. Never give that Prizzi look!' – Prizzi was from American crime fiction, a benevolent gangster figure who in extreme situations produced a 'look'. The call was ineffective in that it hardened their opposition to the man. They wanted to sell the farm and could understand his wish to get into the act and earn some money but there was to be no uncertainty, Ronald was the agent and all potential purchasers must

speak to him. He was free to negotiate a fee to anyone who introduced a buyer or helped in any way to do so, but that was a matter for him: John should not be involved, especially if there was any dispute over the matter. The old saying was quoted: one did not hire a dog and bark oneself. Hearing this led Charlotte to remark that in a way Ronald did remind her of one, a gun dog, happily sniffing over Bithnie and hoping to come up with what, something making the long flight north?

Walking round the farm with Charlotte the new people showed interest in the woodland and in the beautiful views but not in the growing of crops or quality of the pastures. In the steading the man made one or two comments but none relevant to the cattle or the space available or how the place was used. The woman said very little but took care where she placed beautifully shod feet. It was hard to weigh up whether they were serious.

'I couldn't make them out John, they didn't ask the right questions, not like farmers or would-be farmers. Certainly not like the Brothers. Yet why bother to come?' … The man's tweeds were perfect for the country. His wife was immaculately groomed, her suit a subtle blend of autumn colours was well-cut and had to be expensive. Altogether a mystery why these two should look over Bithnie. Had they ideas other than farming? For example getting permission for building? All in all, breeding and rearing fine stock, the backbone of Scottish farming for long years, seemed highly unlikely for this pair.

'Probably a waste of time. We have to expect that, people looking round but unlikely to go further.'

John's mind was on the Angus calf. He had treated it again with the powder but it would have to come down. The last time he looked the cow had covered its head in sharn. Charlotte was still puzzling and it brought to mind the man who promoted the visit.

103

'Don't forget that beggar would send anybody, parents, grandparents, even their old dog, to keep in ...'

'Mmm. That suit, I wonder if she got it in Inverness, you know that super shop ...' she said absently.

28

A Sorry Hert's Aye Dry

After the 'mystery' pair came a lull when nothing happened, no movement at all. Silence even from the pushy agent. This brought feelings not exactly of depression but close. There was the need to say to all contenders, 'Hey, come on, offer or hop off , we have to know!' The house was immaculate, the farm as orderly as it was possible to be, and no one came, no one looked, no one telephoned for an appointment. Opening the *Press and Journal* and glancing at the horoscopes as people who wholeheartedly deride them often do, Charlotte noticed the one for John and read it to him: 'You will bring sparkle to all around you ...'

He was slumped, heavy browed, at the table.

'How long is it going to take?' was the question.

An unexpected response, the coffee mug pushed away, 'I'm going to check a few things. When I get back we're away!'

'But, what if ...?'

'Put your bonnet on!'

Tric-trac, tric-trac over the bridge and a sense of escape. It would do them good to leave everything, cows, telephone, 'that beggar' and all. It was a bright day, cold and crisp and the retirement vehicle was comfortable, gave a smoother ride. They had almost forgotten the neat, swift *Alfa*, the 'red streak' of other days.

105

They headed north.

'I think we may find some sea.'

'How did you guess?'

Lumsden, Rhynie, Huntly, Turriff and then Fraserburgh's harbour, and small fishing boats marked FR but fewer of them. Not much sail, one or two single masted with a mizzen. Big steel trawlers, dark blue or the colour of red lead had patches of rust. All the complicated gear of fishing, nets, spars, lines and ropes, floats made of bright plastic, arc lamps to light the deck at night. Strange aids to navigation out of the landsman's ken. Fishy, tarry smells with the salt tang of the sea, but oil encroaches. The sky cold and clear with a little faint sunshine. Scavenger gulls screaming, swoop on anything; others perched on guard rails or atop masts are edgy and alert; some float quiet on greenish water. Pleasant this scene, but beyond the sheltering walls men know of an unquiet sea as John knew before he took to green fields.

Hot and melting in the mouth, very, very fresh fish and chips the obvious meal before a stroll round and a visit to the ships chandler. Ropes on the farm had come from there; now there was no need for them but a stout basket would be useful anywhere and into the basket went a lightweight rainproof complete with hood ideal for Charlotte in uncertain summers. Home then on narrow roads and through the 'lang toons', their houses stretched out not clustered like the English villages. Light failing as they crossed the bridge, the farm peaceful and welcoming. No sound from the animals, no message waiting from neighbours and none from Ronald. A good day and from it came the resolve to escape again, even if briefly, to have a look and maybe find somewhere to drop anchor after the two of them left the farm road and the clattering bridge to someone else.

They got news of a farmhouse not too far away. A farmer had inherited land but had no need of the house and that

was for sale. On one of the planned forays going to look was no problem, an afternoon off the farm should give enough time. The approach to the place was pleasant with a fair amount of trees. The house had spacious, well-proportioned rooms and good windows. It was very nice indeed but Charlotte was downcast.

'Do you remember a man we met, on the Hamble River? He was refurbishing one of the old sailing ships, can't remember which … He spoke of his wife as little somebody or other? Or she may not have been his wife …'

Vague though this description was, John did remember.

'Yes, As well as the boat he had a lovely old house somewhere and was trying to sell it. Richard, Richard something like Locke, or Luke. I think he called her little Ren, short for René?'

'Well, he told me a famous actor came to look and thought the house perfect, raved about it, wanted immediate possession until walking in the grounds he saw a railway line. Richard explained there was only one train each day and in any case the line was a long way from the house. The old actor was inconsolable, completely put off. Richard had tried again – "Just one in the day and not visible from the house". The famous eyes had closed then wrinkled in despair before the wonderful voice throbbed, "But my dear! Don't you see? I should be waiting for it!"'

The farmhouse adjoined a steading where cows would be fed, and tractors would need access and that made Charlotte think:

'It's like the train John … We would be waiting … at feeding time … worried if they were late …'

'You have a point. We would want to poke our noses in!'

They had built up expectation, maybe because the area was familiar, friends close by. It was disappointing, the house had been right.

'Don't worry, there are plenty of places.'

107

'We can't buy yet in any case.'

'Let's open a bottle when we get home.'

'In a good cause.'

Later that evening a telephone call reinforced the decision to drink the waters of Lethe – the first couple from Wales could not raise the money to buy Bithnie, were very sorry...

29

Sold to the Gentleman From Wales

News of the young couple failing to raise the finance for
Bithnie did not really surprise either John or Charlotte; at
the start it had seemed unlikely when the wife voiced doubts
not only about money but of being able to manage a bigger
enterprise.

'The woman had the last word!'

'You nearly said as usual.'

'Would I dare!'

In any case farm business now took prominence, the
forward steers were to go to market and preparation for this
exodus began. First the animals were contained in the
nearest place to the door where six at a time could be filtered
into an outside pen and then into the waiting float. An early
start and the inevitable sinking of the heart at parting with
creatures born on the farm, reared and cared for through all
manner of ills. Charlotte had adapted well to farming,
unfazed by many things and stoic about others but this for
her was the nadir, in all the years endured with a heavy heart.
In truth John had the worst of these times, having to plan
and execute the move, follow and supervise the animals'
housing at the Mart, then watch the whole process of selling.
His feelings were the same as Charlotte's but better hidden.
From time immemorial animals had been raised for
slaughter to ensure survival for the human race but in the

present phase of existence people were questioning, rejecting meat and finding other food. What would be the fate of animals if all people did the same? No easy answer to that one.

The aim at Bithnie was good husbandry followed by the swift transit from farm to sale, giving all effort to reduce stress. In a poem called 'The Bell' the doctor-poet David Rorie wrote 'Bide, lippen, thole, lippen, thole, bide' which seemed apt to Charlotte, the present move being the last time for them to 'thole' anything at all to do with forward steers.

A day or two later the telephone rang to give news from the second Welsh couple and Charlotte had answered. John was talking to Stuart who had brought a selection of Sunday papers to keep them in touch with a world of strange people who did not farm. They had chatted over coffee and now Stuart was about to drive his Range Rover away down the road.

'John. More bad news. That was Eddie. He can't pay what he thinks is our bottom line. Is about £5,000 short!'

There passed between the two men a look that Neanderthal man might have exchanged with his best Neanderthal hunting pal.

'Hmm … What did you say to him?'

'Oh, just that I was sorry, they seemed so keen on the farm. And that I hoped he would find somewhere eventually.'

A pause before a question from Stuart, considered and courteous as always: 'You don't think he was, as we might say, takkin' the lift? Awarding himself a wee discoont?'

'More than likely but Charlotte would never see it. Not in a million years!'

It was incautious. The look he received was similar to Neanderthal woman's, the one given before she stomped off to fling a tree-trunk on the fire. As things turned out it was fortunate that Charlotte had taken the call and so readily

believed what Eddie said because the next day saw a complete *volte-face*. The sale was on, at a figure John could accept, with no 'discoont'. The following weekend Eddie would arrive to discuss details but in the meantime would notify the agent, the solicitors and all concerned in Wales. *Fait accompli?*

Well, these things are never truly ac-compli-shed until the contract is signed but without people coming to look at the house there could be less dusting and polishing, the Sunday newspapers and other things could lie around without being swept away out of sight; in fact life would be more normal. Finding somewhere to live had more urgency and with fewer mouths to feed after the exodus of steers it was easier to take time to explore further. The search was on.

A neighbour told them of an acquaintance who wanted to sell his house in Aberdeen. The man was an academic, recently widowed, who had moved to a more suitable modern flat. He was a doctor of something or other but not a medical one. There was attraction in the complete contrast of living in a city after so many years 'at the back o' beyont': doctor and dentist easy of access, a railway station and freedom to go anywhere in the country, visit old friends and new places. With supermarkets handy no need to buy in vast quantities of food, a freezer was hardly necessary. The house had to be worth a look.

Built of the ubiquitous grey granite it was impressive. Three floors; a second door indicated a separate garden flat. A patch of lawn and one or two shrubs had the minimal look favoured by someone who was busy elsewhere. Doctor X opened the door. He was tall, rather languid and uncertain of where to start showing the house. It became clear that they were the first to view and he was vague about curtains and carpets and whether the light fittings were to be included in the sale. In their turn, the two farmers were at a loss when it came to asking the questions. They had lived for so many

111

years at a distance from other people it was hard to imagine what living in this place would be like. As they looked out, a man was working in the next door garden which was not at all minimal. This brought neighbours to mind, close neighbours, something a couple of near-eremites would have to get used to. John narrowly missed asking about the 'neipers' saying instead, 'Is he from next door?' The answer was laconic: 'Yes. That is Mr Brown.'

At Burnside Charlotte had been introduced to a Mr Bruin whom she addressed as such many times before realising that he was Mr Brown.

'And what is Mr Brown like?' she asked carefully.

Doctor X raised an eyebrow and puckered his mouth.

'What is he like ...?' after a long minute the answer came:

'He plays golf. He is a keen golfer.'

It did not seem worth knowing more of a neighbour so lacking in complexity. They followed their host upstairs to see his sitting room. Large, with elegant proportions, it was spoiled by a wood-burning stove not in itself ugly though out of character. More offensive to the eye were tiles on the walls around the stove. Roughly made and not well-fixed, in raw colours clashing with everything in the room, the tiles invited the response 'One of us must go!' that Oscar Wilde as he lay dying gave to the wallpaper in his room. Warmed by his giant stove, the doctor poring over his books and papers seemingly did not mind, or, dread thought, were they chosen on some foreign tour, his spoils, in the same vein as the Elgin Marbles? Viewing the rest of the house Charlotte could not forget, kept looking for tiles, as if the originals had darkly multiplied and made invasion into every room.

On the return journey to the back of beyond, John offered, 'I know what you thought about the sitting room but things could be changed.'

And that was true, It would be pleasant to refurbish such a house but another truth was that it was a great deal bigger

112

than they needed, might give them problems they could do without; they wanted space but not quite so much of it.

It was interesting to have a visit from the friend who had told them of the granite house. They gave an account but did not describe the sitting room décor. By way of light relief they mentioned Mr Brown of whom there was nothing to say except that he played golf. Mrs Mack's reaction surprised them. With some disapproval and perhaps a smidgeon of relish she relayed the spik: 'Yon chiel may hiv nae thing te say aboot Mr Bruin bit he kens Mrs Bruin weel eneuch. Took her to the new hoose! She bides theeir!'

Bidey-eens had a certain fascination. Within days of arriving in Scotland the postie had informed that a certain rich lady, sadly widowed, had acquired one to share her magnificent house not far away. That one was of course male but there were later females like the doctor's Mrs Brown. Young, middle-aged or rather old, there seemed no age limit, just a quiet proliferation of the habit. Later Charlotte was told that the term 'dyke-lowper' describing a cow given to jumping over obstacles could also be applied to a man who disregarded the commandment about coveting his neighbour's wife. It was all recorded in the richness of the Doric.

After the Aberdeen house, 'neipers' became rather more significant when considering where to live. You had to be aware of trends.

30

All is For the Best

The weekend arrived and so did the people from Wales. They had come all the way with only short stops and looked jaded, particularly Eddie's father who was 80 years old. They sat in the kitchen at Bithnie waiting for coffee to burble up on the Aga, not willing to be rushed into inspecting the farm as Eddie plainly wanted.

The parents-in-law were eager to approve: Mother was explicit: 'Yes. No doubt at all they are lucky to have this chance so young, indeed they are. But Eddie is such a worker hardly ever still and our girl was brought up the same as we were ourselves and of course we are behind them not only with money but in every way, spending time here God willing, and Dai turns his hand to anything. We are one hundred per cent certain they will make a go of it and Eddie's Da thinks the same ...'

In the pause for breath the old man settled deep in John's chair nodded, smiling at his son and then nodded to John and Charlotte to confirm. It became evident that all three were going to back the venture with a good deal of money. They were nice people and their trust in Eddie was touching.

'Better giving it now, see? Than waiting ...'

Dad had a point there.

After sandwiches and cake the party was ready to go with John round the farm. The young folk had told the tales but

this was reality: the parents were ready to admire every inch of Bithniet to see the words made flesh.

Charlotte had felt uncomfortable with money talk and at the same time a reluctant admiration for the uninhibited frankness shown. To her, things of that sort were between you and if not your Maker then certainly your banker and John was of the same mind. She cleared the table and put things ready for another meal and although they had decided to sell and knew it was sensible, felt depressed. In her heart of hearts she did not want to leave Bithnie, would like to say to the nice Welsh family, 'Sorry! Change of mind!' or in the vernacular 'Steek the door ahin ye!' She knew how absurd that was.

Back in the house the family was radiant with approval, everything was fine, in particular the stock. Again Mother put it into words: 'This is a truly bewtiful place. Lovely it is! You have some bewtiful animals and I guarantee you won't go wrong handing them over to our young people; they will carry on just the same with the same high standards, you may count on that.'

More discussion. More of the capabilities of Eddie and his young wife and eventually a decision to set off on the long journey home. Another visit planned and a tentative date for the final handover before cordial goodbyes. At last just the two of them left clearing the debris of the meal. John could read the signs.

'Don't say it!' Be like Dr Pangloss – everything happens for the best!'

'And don't you forget that in the end he only said it, didn't believe it any more!'

'At least we shall have less work. Some comfort in that.'

Charlotte felt the need to get out of the house:

'Can you bear another hike?'

They went into the quiet of the wild wood but even there, a question. Would Eddie keep this place unspoiled, leave it

green and secret or perish the thought would new brooms 'swype clean', make tidy, fill holes where trees had fallen, use their wood for winter fires? Here a white pheasant picked a wary way and Charlotte thought of the Holy Ghost; small creatures walked undisturbed, had shelter in plenty. They strolled back pausing at the river's edge where the cattle drank and the wide path smelled of them. There was no challenge from the water, smooth and gently flowing on its way. In spate the Don was frightening enough to cause panic when young stock crossed an old fence to get a better bite. Trying to get them back had in fact made things worse, the frisky young things more in danger of falling into the water as they dodged. Now the fences were renewed but memories were everywhere and could not be dodged. Back along known paths, through the strong gates made by the Monymusk Lad, a peep into the steading to see what was going on there and then the only possible end to the day, more water, a good dram of the water of life.

31

North and South

A local preacher known as 'Gallopin' Tam' delivered the same sermon as he visited all the parishes in his care and this did not go unnoticed, was recorded in a rhyme. Preaching about the widow's cruse he went,

> Up by Tough an doon by Towie
> He preached the wifie an her bowie
> In Forbes, Keig an Tullynessle
> 'Twas aye the wifie an her vessel,
> Up by Rhynie, doon Strathbogie
> 'Twas aye the wifie an her cogie,
> Aa through Cabrach an Strathdon,
> Aye he preached the wifie on,
> Aa the fowk roon Craigievar
> Kent the wifie an her jar …

After the visit of Eddie's family when the need for somewhere to live became more urgent they began to feel kinship with Tam as with one thought in mind they covered his ground … Skene … Peterculter … Turra … Meldrum … and the rest. Over the days they managed to look and they did see nice houses within their means but lacking something, a view, easy access, sufficient land. Some were too small or too ugly, some too big, particularly a good manse house at Keig.

117

John thought it pointless to take on too many rooms: he hated the sound of the vacuum cleaner and was aware that Charlotte would be zealous. Charlotte did not like dormer windows and sloping bedroom ceilings and these found in most small houses were 'claustrophobic'. And wallpaper: 'It might be the same as the green paint'. In past times paint sold by a slick salesman had spread its nasty tegument year on year over all the local sitting rooms, blunting aesthetic sense. That was a theory dreamed up by Charlotte and now she added wallpaper to the bargain offers, warning that people offered rampant roses and strange colours should think twice, 'be wary', as recommended by the bard.

They had second thoughts about city living as too great a contrast after the wide open spaces of the farm and the three storeys of the Aberdeen house were too much anyway. They went to Inverness, then eastwards to Nairn, Forres, Elgin and along the coast to villages picturesque in summer sun yet in winter huddled close with the nuance of communities sufficient unto themselves, where an incomer might feel unwelcome. It would have been nice to be near the sea but some northerly places were so far off the beaten track that easy travel from there seemed unlikely. Another look at Frazerburgh, more fish and chips but no suitable houses. They would next go south.

After a day or two, with arrangements with Wullie to stay on the farm for the day, they went across the Potarch Bridge and over the Cairnomounth, planning to stop at the highest point to eat sandwiches and have coffee. It proved to be a brilliant idea, the view truly magnificent. Stepping from the vehicle they found the wind sharp and very cold, making them gasp and huddle into coats, buttoning the collars. But it was exhilarating.

'Don't waste this! Fill your lungs!' John was ever conscious of pure air. Breathing deep, in that high place the problems of a house-hunt became trivial, the moment sufficient unto itself.

In the patterned world far below a fitful sun showed here and there some hint of gold soon snatched by swift shadow and hustled away over endless hills to blur at last into the wide arc of sky.

It was hard to leave that cold high place.

They moved on first in the direction of Fettercairn, to Edzell, skirting Brechin and on the A94 into Dundee. A long, long bridge over the Tay, a sight of the rail bridge and an attempt to remember William McGonagall's lines about the terrible disaster in the early days of rail:

> Beautiful Railway Bridge of the Silv'ry Tay!
> Alas, I am very sorry to say ...
> That ninety lives have been taken away ...

After that a short drive to reach St Andrews. They had discussed this university town, thinking it could offer a good deal of what they wanted; at any rate it had to be explored. Cars were double-parked on the main street with motorists hovering to fill any space made vacant. Apparent control by displaying a ticket which could be purchased, but where? A passer-by, a civil man who touched his cap to Charlotte thereby gaining approval, pointed to a shop not far away. It was simple if you knew.

In addition to splendid ruins, a wide stretch of sandy shore and the renowned golf course, St Andrews had three streets for the business of the town, one mainly for the university, the others for shops, a really good fishmonger and almost next door an excellent butcher, both with customers having to queue. A fine display outside the greengrocer's, many bread and tea shops and a smallish Marks & Spencer. A proliferation of three commodities, tartan, woollens and golf paraphernalia was not surprising when you gave it a thought. And yet, so many clubs, bags, balls; so much 'designer' gear with matching caps, sweaters with or without diamond

patterns, special shoes with flaps to cover the laces, golf trolleys, buggies, lessons, coaching, this was a world unknown to anyone thinking the development of the ball was a mistake. There was art for sale, modern and the more traditional, in one shop Victorian paintings of hill and glen. Bookshops and the resolve to take time for books after calling on every estate agent in sight.

It appeared that in St Andrews itself little that appealed was for sale. Old, beautiful houses were occupied, their owners snug and settled. Each agent spoke of houses in new developments outside the town and of others in the small villages on the coast. Without much enthusiasm they accepted brochures for these and headed for the bookshops.

John bought a book on Thomas Somerscales, a marine artist, and Charlotte a more modest paperback of the poems of Edwin Muir. They learned from the elderly man behind the counter that Edwin Muir used to patronise the shop and was a pleasant gentle man. He showed less enthusiasm about the poet's wife, implying in the mildest way that Wilma wore the trews.

It was time to go back, with nothing ac-compli-shed regarding a house, but certain refreshment in the change of scene, a pleasant journey and a little knowledge gained about St Andrews. They took a more direct way on major roads, to Arbroath for excellent fish and chips once more and then Stonehaven, the Potarch and the final Alford Bridge.

At one of the brief stops Charlotte thumbed the garnered brochures and said: 'There may be one or two of these we could look at.' To do so would mean another trip.

32

Loose Ends

Before the sale was completed Charlotte had to spend time in the office. It was hard to work up enthusiasm for accounts when anything to do with animals and their welfare, strawing out, feeding, dosing, or doing the usual checks on them was important and much more interesting. From the beginning of farming life she had taken on the bookwork and in time developed a system whereby things were kept fairly up to date. Naturally when any crisis loomed paperwork was left on the desk where it piled up and in some mysterious way multiplied to bring mild despair when it had to be tackled. Sitting at the desk for a final onslaught she was reluctant to start, first tidying the little tray that held pens, pencils and a rubber, then re-reading a letter received that morning from her friend Lisa. Odd scraps of paper went into the wastepaper basket with yesterday's shopping lists. A half-finished crossword caught her eye. It seemed a good idea to put coffee on the stove ready for John. Once before when facing an overflowing in-tray and forms that required information not easy to come by she had written in the diary something of *a cri de coeur.* 'Will no one rid me of this burden of paperwork? No sooner do I believe I am clear than the hordes attack again!'

This time it was different because when the final t was crossed and last i dotted the VAT book could gather mildew

waiting the relevant number of years in some as yet unknown house.

The Min. of Ag. having concerns only with Eddie as the owner of Bithnie would give no more than a perfunctory wave as she and John walked off into the sunset. It was strange and hard to acknowledge.

She picked up a lengthy letter from the Regional Council about Bithnie Hill, Forest of Tornashean but the euphony of the heading did not make for a general clarity: an attached form stated 'You will be required…' Unwilling to be required the file labelled 'Pending' was appropriate. The account book would be easier, entering receipts which were few and the expenses always high.

She remembered buying the first account book: they had looked at different ones not knowing what was suitable for an undertaking of less than global importance, yet it mattered very much to them, they wanted to get it right. They settled on a Collins Cathedral Analysis Book with a cheerful red cover.

T.S. Eliot in the guise of *Alfred J. Prufrock* wrote 'I have measured out my life with coffee spoons'. Charlotte turned pages in the red book to see: 'Paid by CASH', 'Paid by CHEQUE' and the details, 'Anderson, Mackie, Ogden, Norvite, Low, HydroElectric, Williamson, HM Customs (VAT), page after page of bounty given. Similarly 'Kept in CASH', Paid to BANK', HM Paymaster-General, Aberdeen & N. Marts, Hamlyns, Ministry of Agriculture. Fewer items entered here.

A lot of money recorded in columns headed feed, straw, manures, seeds, fuel, light, vet, medical, repairs. Other amounts shown under plant, equipment, minerals, loose tools – she never understood them – how did a tool become loose? Detached from what? She remembered a teacher saying, 'Form yourselves into loose groups' and how she and the other girls had fallen about laughing. And now the tools were in loose groups.

From day one between the covers of the Cathedral Analysis Books the minutiae of their farming life was recorded, measured out ... How scrupulous she had been at first, afraid that the odd personal expense would creep into the farm stuff; later she thought it funny when a diligent VAT lady pointed to a tube of toothpaste hidden among farm supplies. In addition she had forgotten to make an adjustment for personal telephone calls. Tut! Tut! However, the VAT lady's car became stuck when she reversed into the quagmire of a farm gateway and had to be retrieved by a certain knight in a John Deere tractor. Nothing more was heard of the errors made by the parfit gentil knyght's lady-wyfe.

All in all things had been straightforward with few mistakes or misunderstandings. Officials had been courteous and helpful and some became friends. She believed they were considered good payers who dealt promptly with accounts sent but then again did a faint suspicion linger about that other life of theirs when they were rich. If only ...

33

Crawlers

A cow called Jilly reminded them that drama was never far away where cattle are concerned. It seemed like the middle of the night when John was awakened by harsh repetitive noise, the sound of distress. Fuddled by sleep he knew it was all a mistake, animals would be lying in deep straw, most of them sleeping, the odd one licking her calf, drowsy and contented. It was just one of those very real dreams he had, being obsessed ... But Charlotte was alert – 'John, there's a cow, listen ...'

It did not take long to get over to the steading and strangely to draw a blank. No movement: the air heavy with the sweet smell cows have, and more strongly than in daytime, the old stones breathing their essence of time past. There was no need to switch on lights to disturb that peace. They left quickly when the sound, starting again, led them to the Dutch barn and Jilly.

She was standing in front of high-piled bales of hay, the hoarded winter food. Not far away the grey gander stretched his neck from side to side, hissing in defence of his dames, huddled together babbling nervousness. The cow lifted her throat to make the sound again, but hoarseness diminished it to a pitiful croak; she had bawled too long.

'Oh lassie, poor lassie ...' Charlotte reached up and was angrily thrust off, the cow butted against a bale and came

away garlanded with a remnant of summer. John was on his knees shining the torch to find space between the piles – there must somewhere be a calf, dead or alive.

'You think ...?'

'Without a doubt! She's telling us. But how we find out ...'

Charlotte looked. 'If ever we needed a small Japanese!' She realised that she would have to try; John would get stuck. She dreaded confined spaces, was the last person on earth ... but what was the alternative? The thought of the stifling bales closing in on her made for panic, her throat so dry when she spoke it was like Jilly's croak.

'Give me the torch!'

Pushing past the first bales was not too bad, the next were so close she had to turn and ease herself through on one shoulder. For a moment she thought of going back, it was simply no place to be, not fair, not worth the risk with all the looming bales. One more push and then perhaps a rest and rethink ... comfort from a slightly wider space and then the torch showing ... Was that? Could it possibly be? Yes! A tail, a scrap of a tail between the next bales. She had found the calf.

Increased effort to claw through, to reach and check. Had it driven further and further into the mass of bales, lost sense of direction, panicked and eventually given up? Was the tail attached to a living, breathing body? Half a minute to see a creature oblivious to his mother's pain or anything else, just solidly asleep, mouth opened on a lolling tongue. Relief made her want to laugh, stifled, squashed and uncomfortable though she was. It was a pity to think of disturbing this sleeping beauty. Aware that if startled he might blunder away from her further into the stack she got an arm beneath the plump warm body and in a strong embrace managed to drag him round to face the way out towards his mama before he was half awake. Prodding at his rump she propelled him forward half crouched at first but he was surprised enough to move quite quickly through the narrow spaces. Pushing and

shoving, prickly with sweat and with loosened hay penetrating every bit of clothing she followed the wanderer back to reality. Light was just appearing ...

'Well done Yoko!' John was pleased, in fact elated, having feared the worst as she had.

The biggest surprise was Jilly. In the first place they had put her in the barn with her calf because of a doubt about their bonding. It was always a good idea to isolate a cow and calf to make sure of this. The violence of Jilly's distress seemed to confirm the bonding yet when the calf went immediately to nuzzle at the bag she backed off, kicking out, unwilling to suckle. It needed John's 'steading' voice, the one used exclusively for cows, before she stood for her prodigal to guzzle away. A lashing tail showed his pleasure.

'Well madam, feed the others now or breakfast?'

'Breakfast, just this once.'

A wicked thought from John – 'There must have been a million creepy crawlies in there, biting ones! Have a good look!'

'I'll tak a bath an' they'll jis droon!'

34

East Neuk

One or two things had to be sorted out before they could leave the farm and cross the Cairnomounth on the way to the unexplored villages beyond St Andrews. John and Charlotte had decided that because the cows were hefted to the land they would offer them to Eddie at a reasonable price and would walk 'doon the road' themselves rather than send the herd to market. Valuations were needed of all livestock, of quantities of hay, straw, manures and a vast conglomeration of farm stuff piled up in the steading and other buildings. The worth of re-seeded pasture land must be calculated as first year and so on. The amount realised from these assets was to figure in the final accounts. A question had been raised about the farm's water supply: samples were sent for analysis and an estimate sought for the provision of main drainage, but that was a matter for Eddie and was left in his hands.

Thus several days passed before the home search began again. As before the cows and Bithnie were left in capable hands and quite early in the day two almost-retired farmers were at the high point of the journey. Still magnificent the wide sweep of the land, the farms and the few clustered houses, but a sky heavy with cloud, no transient gold lost to shadow, the hills less distinct and colour gone. Again, the high place had an effect, left them relaxed and hopeful.

St Andrews and soon past the university to find the coast road. First to Crail, very old and picturesque with a tiny harbour almost silted up, hinting at more active times. Anstruther next, with attractive boats and the salt smell of the sea enhanced by a bracing wind. A holiday air in the long street busy with shoppers. Into a tiny restaurant for more of the staple diet for house-hunters before a short drive to the next port of call, Pittenweem, with many seagoing trawlers and a lot of activity around the harbour. Of immediate interest a FOR SALE notice in the window of a house on the seafront. In an office a few doors away a tall thin man uncoiled himself from behind a desk which almost filled the very small room. The solicitor/agent was ready to chat, perhaps glad to leave paperwork piled on the desk. He listened to their query and was apologetic: 'I am sorry, that one's gone, went straight away, the notice should have been taken down.'

He mentioned other houses but questioned: 'If I may be inquisitive, tell me, is your furniture fairly big? I imagine it might be, in a farmhouse. You will get a shock seeing how tiny the rooms are in old houses like this – I haven't room to swing a cat and all three floors are the same. They used to house fisherfolk with big families all crammed in somehow. Admittedly they're picturesque but in my opinion you would be disappointed.'

They talked for a while and took brochures he offered in his capacity as estate agent: some of them they already had, from the first trip to St Andrews.

They moved on to St Monans and parked on a small patch of rough ground near the harbour. On the narrow road the small houses had the look of places lost to their original use. Painted in pastel colours, with gleaming white paint, shining doorknockers and bright flowers these were charming homes but the owners were unlikely to make a living from fishing.

A lively breeze made it impossible to read the latest brochures except inside the car. In some discomfort they tried to spread them out to compare with those from St Andrews and riffled through them all to find something of interest. They checked on a place Charlotte had picked out but found it was the only house on a side road and had a forlorn look. Far from solitary, another house was in a cluster, all at strange angles to one another, the tiny patches of garden oddly overlapping. The brochure had pictures of charming rooms with quaint beamed ceilings and an inglenook fireplace but John could not persuade Charlotte to consider it.

'No good. I couldn't. Such a huddle ... you must see it would be like living in a goldfish bowl!'

'No chance of topless sunbathing, I admit!'

Back to the car and another look at the papers which had to be the last as time was running out.

A brochure from St Andrews was now incomplete, the type indistinct, the pictures adrift.

'We might as well look at this one, it isn't modern, says "period".'

It was at the top of the hill leading to the harbour and house and garden were hidden by a very high wall. A gable end was the only interruption to the wall which continued until it reached the next house on a street adjoining the hill. House and garden were thus shut off and did not conform to the pattern of tall, narrow houses there.

They peeped through a wrought iron gate and saw a concreted yard and a tree: from the hill they had looked up to see branches reaching towards the light. They went to the door of the house and knocked but there was no answer. Repeated knocking and no reply encouraged them to take a look. In the yard a small stone building, its windows grey and cobwebbed, was like a farm bothy. Along a side path to the front of the house, where they stood transfixed. This house

on the hill had a vista of sky and sea which took the breath away. Only a perfunctory mention of the view over harbour and sea had been written in the brochure.

It felt strange and wrong to peer through windows to see inside the house but only through a glass oval in the stout front door did they get any clear picture. A wrought iron balustrade with a polished wooden handrail curved to a high window halfway up a wide stone stairway.

They had to go. It was well past time to start the return journey. For some time they were silent, trying to decide on the next step; it was obvious that the house had to be visited again, with permission to view.

35

A Dream of a Church

The St Monans house was the sort of place they had in mind, of the right size and nice-looking with the wonderful view of the harbour and sea and yet before making an arrangement to see it again they had misgivings. Detached, with a garden, it was at the corner of a mainly terraced street. Was it the right house but in the wrong place? They were used to having a good deal of space for the business of farming and mostly they worked without other people being involved. Had they become too absorbed, concentrating too much on the farm and neglecting the social side of things?

> I wish I loved the human race,
> I wish I loved its silly face,
> I wish I liked the way it walks,
> I wish I liked the way it talks,
> And when I'm introduced to one
> I wish I thought 'What Jolly Fun!'

Written by Sir Walter Raleigh long after his ancestor brandished a cloak to keep a queen's feet dry, the amusing doggerel came to mind and Charlotte thought it might be apt for them. Without realising it they had become reclusive. Typical of John, the quick denial.

Everyone knew and would tell her what a people-lover he

131

was ... 'as long as they kept at a reasonable distance of course.'

Time was pressing. Eddie, anxious to complete the sale, was telephoning daily, planning, questioning, sometimes just chatting, referring to the farm as 'mine' or 'ours'. Like it or not, he was assuming ownership of Bithnie and they had to gather up belongings and make way.

At St Monans the agent/solicitor acting for the owner, who lived and worked in Edinburgh, took them round the house. Simon was enthusiastic about the golden-yellow sandstone, the date 1820 carved above the front door, the house important enough to be mentioned in *The Buildings of Scotland* by John Gifford, published by the National Trust.

'A lot of history here! If you look in the churchyard, one or two very old stones are interesting, particularly John Barron's, who built this house.'

Whether Simon was a historian or merely an astute salesman did not matter, they were intrigued. They studied a new brochure:

> ... the house occupies a superb setting overlooking St Monans to the harbour and sea below and enjoys fine southerly views to the Bass Rock and Berwick Law in East Lothian. This area of Fife, known as the East Neuk, is renowned for its lovely coastal scenery and as well as St Monans includes the traditional fishing villages of Crail, Pittenweem, Anstruther and Elie ... St Monans itself having a most beautiful harbour.
> ... from the hall a curved stone staircase with wood panelling, ornate metal balustrades and rosewood handrail leads to the landing with large Georgian window ... ornate cornices, dado ... a stone-built outbuilding, two-storey, with mains water and electricity.

The rooms in the house were smaller than the outside

appearance suggested, with one exception: an upstairs sitting-room was spacious and had a breathtaking view of the sea. A disappointment was a banal tiled fireplace. The hall and curved stone stairway were even better than in the first glimpse. As if in a Victorian painting a calm sea was visible through the oval window in the front door.

Simon locked up and said goodbye. His face had the bland expression of a man who suspected he had sold a house. Indeed, all that remained was the decision. A Rubicon confronted them and they had to decide whether to make the crossing.

'Have we time?' As always they had to get back to the cows but they could not resist a quick visit to the churchyard to look for the gravestone of the man who built the house on the hill. It took only minutes but when they found the stone so old and crumbling was it that the words were difficult to read and fading light warned that they should be on their way, back to the farm and possible crises arising from their absence. Charlotte scribbled what they could make out, first what seemed to be high praise of John Barron's wife, AGNES GRAY who died aged 67 in 1851. There was also JOHN BARRON ESQ. his date obscure, and 'her(?) FATHER and MOTHER and DAVID, father of the above JOHN BARRON are buried here'.

They followed the same route, stopping for a fish supper in Arbroath before the long drag north, then at last the clattering brig told the cows that the boss was home, would look them over and maybe give a morsel of hay to last them until morning. When finally John and Charlotte climbed the stair the house and St Monans were gaining favour. The harbour and the sea of course appealed strongly and there was much else of interest. Places in the East Neuk seemed unspoiled as if left behind by modern-day processes. More particularly it would be nice to find out about John Barron and how he came to build his house.

Before Charlotte slept she thought of the tiny church and was puzzled by a sense of having seen or heard of it before. A quiet sea had lapped rocks below the wall round the church and the salt tang was in the air and on the skin, almost to be tasted as they lingered and light faded. It would not always be calm there, the sea would challenge and winds batter the ancient stones. Something she had read … She woke from a dream in which she had been walking towards the church and calling out a name, Margaret, again and again, Margaret … It was odd the way the mind worked, remembering for you while you slept. *The Forsaken Merman*! A poem about a mortal who married a merman and went to live beneath the salt sea. It was graphic: at Easter time the mortal hears church bells and sighs – 'I lose my poor soul Merman here with thee' – goes up through the surf and does not return. The Merman waits for a long time then takes their children with him to the church. They hear the murmur of folk at their prayers as they stand outside. They climb on the graves and they see her, Margaret … They plead but her eyes are on the Holy Book. 'Loud prays the priest; Shut stays the door'. They have to go back 'Down, down, down! Down to the depths of the sea.'

Margaret lives, grateful for the sun, and the priest, the bell and the holy well, but sometimes 'there breaks a sigh and anon there drops a tear from a sorrow-clouded eye and a heart sorrow-laden'. She sighs for 'the cold strange eyes of a little Mermaiden and the gleam of her golden hair' …

Wind, salt tides and a little grey church on a windy hill: as in the poem but it was unlikely Matthew Arnold had been to St Monans. What John would describe as something of a longshot. However, one day she would look to see if a stone for Margaret was there, somewhere near John Barron.

134

36

Warslin' Awa

So that was it. St Monans and the house there. A matter for solicitors to put forward an offer, a wait to see if this was acceptable to the owner, followed by searches into mysteries where only the legal hand dabbles with confidence. In the spik of the North-East advice is to 'Tak a pint an' agree' rather than 'gie muckle siller' to the lawyers, yet with house buying there is no choice but to look happy while the processes reach completion. John's solicitor was a 'Writer to the Signet' which sounded strange and exotic to English ears. Soon this gentleman telephoned a word of caution with information that the man whom they thought to be the owner of the house was in fact part-owner, needing power of attorney from another part-owner who was in hospital. This caused a sinking of the heart for the co-owners of Bithnie and of course delay while it was looked into. Charlotte pictured the scene: a pale figure supine but not *in extremis,* a cluster of interested parties, frowning, hopeful or in the case of the lawyers carefully neutral in an agonising wait before the declaration in a faint, clear voice. This image owed something to a televised production of *Brideshead Revisited* with the wonderful Chinese Room and Sir Laurence Olivier in a magnificent bed. She conceded, 'Yes, of course it would be plainer but the same result, relief all round!'

After a date was fixed with Eddie for their exit from

Bithnie, peace of mind vanished for the farmers.

The business of transferring most of the animals and machinery, disposing of what was neither to be given or sold to Eddie or taken to St Monans, emptying and cleaning out the buildings and tackling the paperwork involved gave no respite. All this had to be done after the routines of the farm, the tractorwork handling bales, the feeding, inspections and treatments. People say moving house is stressful, but a farm? Their friend Wullie knew all about it – 'Preen back yer lugs,' he told them.

As is the way of things a drainage problem arose in one of the parks adjoining the river; after heavy rain several shallow pools appeared and did not drain away. The place had always given trouble because it had a wide dip where the pools gathered. The rest of the field lacked any slope and slow-moving water caused a build-up of silt which eventually blocked the system. John checked outlets on the river bank and cleared weeds and summer growth but the pools did not diminish leaving no alternative but to dig three or four deep holes diagonally across the field. Water welling up in these made it unpleasant having to go in with draining rods, poking and shoving to dislodge whatever was causing the blockages. No one from the other life could have recognised the apparition in waders, mud-covered, grim-faced as hours went by with no success. Was this the gent suited by Chester Barry? The one described as 'dapper'? After more slog and some language familiar on mess-decks throughout Her Majesty's Navy, at last came the relief of water trickling away and the disappearance of the tell-tale pools. Mentioning to Stuart the nuisance of it, the hours spent getting the water drained away into the river, brought a comment: 'As long as I can mind there's been a problem – naeb'dy yet has managed to git the water to flow uphill!'

They made the last batch of young stock ready for the Mart making sure they had retained the tags essential for

136

identifying them. Handling an unwilling animal to give the momentary discomfort of a new tag is not like tagging him when he is newborn: the farmer too suffers his discomforts, kicks and bruises are the norm and giving chase up a steep brae reminds him he is 'nae sae young' as he used to be. As if in tribute to a good life spent on Bithnie this floating was accomplished without drama, no panic, no last-minute refusal to go up the ramp into the float, no banging about, no protest. It was the best and worst of departures and sent Charlotte rushing away into the house, unable to bear the knowledge that this was the forerunner ...

John disliked the business of selling at the Mart. Had it been possible he would have kept animals on the farm 'from cradle to grave' but had found this impractical and resorted to selling forward stores as the next best thing. At this final sale the bidding for Bithnie animals was brisk, in particular for some exceptionally good specimens which two men seemed determined to have. Telling Charlotte afterwards John said, 'I couldn't believe it really, there was a sort of hush as the bidding got really high.' It was a kind of swansong for Bithnie, achieving the highest price of the day. 'Top of the sale' recorded the *Press and Journal* for the enlightenment of all in the Howe and beyond.

'We're going to need a file marked 'Nostalgia' I think,' said Charlotte, reaching for the scissors.

They squeezed in another trip south, viewed the world from high on the Cairnomounth once more before speeding down to St Monans and their future home. Keys had been left with two ladies who lived across the road and judging by conversations on the telephone they would be very pleasant neighbours. Jean and Margaret insisted on making tea for them after the journey. Neighbours mentioned as Aileen and Chrissie gave a greeting and smiled as they crossed over to the house. The village seemed to be a friendly place.

It was interesting exploring the house without anyone else

137

there and it was as pleasant as they remembered. They made plans to replace the tiled fireplace with something in character: places in Edinburgh specialised in the refurbishment of Georgian houses, they would look for something suitable. The time passed quickly but before they left there was a strange telephone call ...

37

Tyauve and Tears

A Blonde-Acquitaine bull borrowed from a neighbour was the next to go from Bithnie. Persuaded to make a quiet exit by quantities of beet nuts, he walked into the horsebox without fuss and it could be said that he more than filled it. When the ramp was lifted and the door shut, giant Tommy realised he had been conned and he objected. His protest was not quiet and continued down the road, over the bridge and probably all the way home. Apart from the tension arising from handling such a powerful creature, Tommy's departure caused little regret; during his brief stay on the farm they had not managed the rapport coming from long association with an animal, caring for him, feeding him, treating his ills and thereby gaining his trust. They were grateful for Tommy's presence and hopeful of the results for Eddie's sake. Truth to tell he had now and again alarmed Charlotte by pawing the ground, scattering missiles of turf behind him, while fiercely jerking his head up and down if she got too near: sometimes it seemed unwise to linger.

Eddie had raised queries about the bridge and John promised to do something about places where sleepers showed signs of wear. Finding someone able to do a repair was a problem until eventually the firm of Anderson of Clatt took on the job, suggesting that by laying planks lengthwise

over the athwartship ones, the whole gained strength and would need little attention for some time to come.

'Anderson of Clatt. That name has a certain ring to it,' observed Charlotte. 'You could guess they would do a good job.' John made no comment having lived with Charlotte for many years.

The first person to cross the refurbished bridge was Margaret from Burnside and she came with a gift of delicate table mats, each with a napkin slotted ingeniously into one corner. Brought back from holiday travelling, they were for the new life in the house at St Monans. Such a charming idea, a civilised taking of tea, no more hurried bites at a sandwich, no gulping and slurping at a hot cup but a leisurely process during an idle afternoon in the garden overlooking the sea. Hard to visualise in the present hassle. Using the pretty blue mats would bring to mind Margaret, John and Dugald, the unique world of Burnside and the distant gleam of Lochnagar. The reality of giving up the farm became more apparent when good wishes and promises to keep in touch came day after day. Left out of reckoning was the good side of retirement, freedom from the strain of heavy work, from worry about animals, weather, overdraft. They wondered what on earth had made them decide to sell when they were not old enough to give up the ghost, become quitters, that was the word for them. Something of confirmation came when they collected bales from a farm owned by two spritely old boys who insisted on carrying and loading them on to the cart. In conversation it emerged that the twins were in sight of their eighty-first birthdays.

To add to the general gloom they discovered at the far end of the farm one of the heifer calves in a very poor state. Given a glucose drink it revived but could not stand. It was vital to take the poor creature back to the steading for treatment and shelter so John hurried to get the tractor. Spreading out a sheet of strong plastic they rolled the inert lump onto it and

with more difficulty onto a pallet. Driving slowly forward he slotted the tines into the pallet and lifted, but immediately lowered again. 'It won't work,' he said. 'It's going to roll off!' Charlotte knew what was coming – 'Jump on and hold her!' he instructed and Charlotte obeyed without any certainty that she would be there when the steading came in view. It was part and parcel of the job, of the farming life, the reason why she had grey hair. The machine began to climb the slope with Charlotte draped over the calf, clinging on for dear life. Wild swings from side to side and spine-jerking bumps somehow did not dislodge the calf or Charlotte and lessened when they reached the fairly level path at the top of the park. The mother had grazed, seeming indifferent as they handled the calf but when the tractor moved away she followed, bellowing distress at the kidnap. At each opened gate John drove through, stopped, waited for the cow before closing and securing the strong gate with a chain. This was repeated three times. Charlotte, held aloft with the calf, could do nothing to help. Together, cow and calf were housed in the bull pen vacated by Tommy and endless treatments began. The calf would not suck but sipped a little water from a bucket and took a tiny amount of pot ale. When late that night she dunged it was a hopeful sign. Patient and aware, the cow settled down in the freshly strawed pen and waited. Day after day the efforts continued: the cow was let out to graze but returned and kept vigil. The diary noted the amounts taken of glucose and water, colostrum, milk powder, pot ale, the nibbles of hay. One item read: 'Calf still alive – looked OK early morning but later flopped. Seems to have no ability to move from recumbent position – cannot right herself after flopping over.' Another 'Calf is worse.' Next day: 'Calf fed dried milk, water, glucose. Looks better.' Later: 'Calf drinking but only desultory picking at food. Given more vitamins. John not happy.' Then: 'Calf fed but prognosis is in question.'

And finally: 'Vet to calf to give fatal injection – a mercy really.' And in large letters '*SUNT LACRYMAE RERUM*'. Wullie said the same thing more or less – 'Ye did yir best John, bit it's aye a bugger fin they dee on ye.'

38

Full Circle

Charlotte did the necessary mucking out of the bull pen, sprayed disinfectant around and was cutting the tow on a bale ready to straw out when she heard the cow at the gate, wanting to return as usual. Ignored, the sounds grew urgent, would go on and on until the voice was a whisper, such is the strength of feeling a cow has for her calf. Understanding came to a halt when all was quiet: did it mean acceptance, or a kinder forgetting? Worse than either would be the stoicism vivid in the Doric 'bide, lippen, thole' but there was no telling.

It would have been nice to take a shower before packing the last of the boxes; maybe after they were filled and sealed with wide sticky tape she would make time. But who was coming up the road in a Range Rover, a different colour from Stuart's? And John was waiting, laughing, shaking someone's hand; two children exploding from the car and more sedately, a woman. It could not be but it was, from the old life the very people who waved them off to Scotland and Burnside, arriving on their last whole day on Bithnie, having no idea that a move was afoot. All those years ago Jean had consoled Charlotte in tears because one of her cats could not be found. Later her husband, also John, would inveigle geese into prepared teachests, cats into travelling baskets and drive them to the airport while John Grey's 'red streak' *Alfa* took to the road 'loaded to the gunwhales' as he described it.

The visit was a flying one, a detour on the way back from buying seed potatoes further north. There was news to catch up on and people, memories of weddings, parties, even of food. Jean remembered fine Stilton and good red wine first sampled at Wellhouse. The little girl listened wide-eyed, her brother cradled in his father's arms dozed while nostalgia reigned. But there were many miles to go for the family – the visit too brief though it was gave great pleasure and something of a rest from the pressure of the move. This time John and Charlotte did the waving off, all the way down the road, and across the bridge before a farewell toot-toot as they gained the road. Later John disclosed that Jean had been worried about Charlotte, said she looked pale and he must make sure she eased off.

'Small wonder!' was the response. 'I feel like a deathshead moth and am probably quite whiffy … but just you wait until I hit the high life of St Monans!'

'I understand that St Monans is called "The Holy City".'

'Not for long!' smirked the deathshead moth.

Just before midnight they went over to the steading. On a last visit Charlotte had imagined lingering in the court, talking to each beast, breathing in all their warmth and sweetness and the very essence of the old place. Disturbed, an owl might leave so softly and so swiftly you had to doubt the glimpse you had. It was not like that. Conscious that the vans would arrive early their need for sleep dulled them but it did not matter. For all time the magic was there in heart and head.

The cows accepted the early feed of double rations given because Eddie would not arrive until much later. As John and Charlotte finished the chore for the last time and came from the steading two vans were trundling over the bridge. From then on things moved at a rate of knots. Four large cheerful men lifted furniture, boxes, tools as if feather-light, slotting them in cleverly to fill every inch of space. After coffee from

the Aga they were away, unfazed that the process would have to be repeated at St Monans.

John had taken the vacuum cleaner from Charlotte saying 'Enough is enough!' As is the case in any removal the house was no longer home as soon as serious preparation began. Now it waited, empty and quiet for others to warm into life. As the Wagen crossed the river there was little sound. It seemed appropriate that with their departure the Bithnie brig no longer clattered its tric-trac.

39

Aftermath

The journey was noticeably quiet. Once Charlotte asked, 'Have you noticed the pattern, as before, but in reverse?'

'Yip!' said John, pushing the Wagen to its maximum speed for a reason he had not yet divulged. A repeat: exactly that. Or the other side of a coin – first many miles towards a farming life and now the miles away from it. Hard physical work should be a thing of the past and weather would hardly concern them. Gone were the days when a downpour of rain spelled disaster. Also lost was the satisfaction of breeding and rearing cattle. As in Whitman's poem, they had looked at them 'long and long' – and found pleasure. On the first journey doubts and fears hardly existed so near were they to their goal: they had land and would become farmers. Should the dream fail they would survive, do something else, change did not alarm them. Pound notes seemed unimportant – what they risked was 'only' money. Now the farming years were at an end, the accounts closed and a line drawn. What was ahead? Only 'God an'the De'il kent!'

The miles wore on. Charlotte's mind went back to the empty farmhouse; how comfortable they had made it, the kitchens retiled, the rest carpeted. They had piled on the logs to make huge fires when the weather was bad, evenings saw them reading or listening to music, the cats shared between them. She sorely missed the cats: Tiger Muffin, Grey

Boy and Blackie, each one a character cat. The farms had given them new lives too and a freedom much relished before they faded into old age … the new place would not have suited them with only a garden and too near a road. She drifted into sleep, trying to think of Eddie and his wife in front of the log fires, with cats and books and music, but they didn't fit and the only chairs she could picture were their own battered old leather ones tight-packed in a van, waiting to be set down in the house by the sea.

The road was a conduit and the Wagen a capsule holding them as if in suspension between two lives, but mile upon mile the strangeness faded, beset by heavy traffic and noise and the need to scrabble for coins to pay the toll across the shining expanse of the Tay.

As expected the vans and the four competent musclemen were waiting and soon house and bothy had either furniture or a plethora of boxes. It was well ac-compli-shed. The two ate hurriedly because John had to return to Bithnie. The previous night he had looked closely at a young heifer and before they left suspected she was fairing to calve. On the journey he had made up his mind to go back. It was something of a shock for Charlotte but she saw the necessity – Eddie would not be in time and John could not leave it to chance even at this late stage. So after food and a short rest, with sleeping bag, pillow and a blanket in the back of the Wagen, John Grey, a farmer for a few more hours, took to the road again.

A woman and a young boy were passing as Charlotte closed the gate after John had driven away. The woman stopped and spoke saying she was glad to see the house occupied again. She was well aware that Charlotte noticed the extraordinary beauty of the child, his large eyes in an olive-tinted face topped by thick dark hair. Charlotte knew of rumours about men from the Spanish Armada leaving their mark all around the coasts of Britain, but no, this was a face from a painting

147

by some old master, the name on the tip of her tongue but she could not remember, would check when books were unpacked.

The next morning after a fitful night in a bedroom full of boxes the metal gate crashed against the wall and high-pitched voices rose from the backyard. Dressing hurriedly Charlotte went to the tall window on the curving stair and saw circling round each other two small boys, angry little boys, strutting in the manner of fighting cockbirds. It was amusing to see they moved forward, made threatening gestures, snarled and spat but never made contact: there was more spin than substance. What astonished Charlotte was recognition of the boy from the painting; there he was, beautiful face contorted, the mouth screaming words to bounce off golden sandstone and slide over the high wall to tell passers-by that John Barron's house was now occupied by less than holy people. The second fechter, fair, rock-solid, his head close-shaven to a pinkish scalp, was equally fluent. How could infants know such words? This had to stop and Charlotte would see to it. She found a voice.

'You are nasty little boys and I want you out of my yard or I'll get the policeman!'

Smartly through the gate and across the road they went as one. Rocky put out his tongue and the painting gave utterance – 'Daft aal bizzom, **** off!'

The gate shut firmly and the bolt slammed across a muttered 'Don't count on it!' … she wished John had seen and heard the diversion.

Due later that day was a visit from a person who telephoned when they first inspected the house as owners. It had been an unpleasant call from someone demanding the return of possessions left in the house, someone obviously at loggerheads with the former owner. The calving heifer had got John off the hook but if the promised visit became awkward she would have to manage. She tried to remember

148

that as well as small locals, she had once separated fighting bulls.

The road back to Bithnie was a weary one with more miles and irritating hold-ups, and cars driven by lunatics. John found the key left for Eddie and went into the house no longer his. In the kitchen he checked the Aga where Charlotte had left food for Eddie and family. She had reminded him to move the casserole from the slow oven to the main one, 'a short time before before you expect them,' He had a look. It smelled delicious – he could have eaten the lot there and then. Knowing himself to be of noble character he made the transfer because surely Eddie would not be long.

Putting in his pocket the lone sandwich uneaten on his journey he crossed to the steading and finding all well there went in search of the heifer. He was right about her. She was going to calve but was taking her time about it. He settled for the long wait, moving now and again, stamping to keep circulation going, and as light faded and it began to rain the calf was born. The heifer licked and cossetted a little bull calf as if following instructions in a manual, a *How to Calve* book.

John felt very pleased about the calf. Always there was a sense of relief and satisfaction when things went well but this was special, the heifer a born mother and Eddie had an extra body. Eddie. Where on earth was he? He quickened pace because the calving had taken so long. And the casserole, he might have jumped the gun with that ...

When he lifted it from an uncommonly hot oven and removed the lid an acrid smell rose from contents once so tempting. What remained was blackened goo, hard-burned, a total ruin. Eddie's supper and his own beyond rescue, *kaput*! He was very hungry and where the hell were they? He gathered up his belongings and went into the dining room to lay out the sleeping bag and pillow, and waited not for Godot

but for bloody Eddie. Wrapped in the blanket he must have dozed before noise on the road. Vans, cars and a trailer pulling another smaller trailer with several dogs. At last! He struggled into his coat and managed to stop the first van where, if Eddie followed instructions, the cows could be unloaded. Wary and blinking against the sudden light, four cows staggered down the ramp into a heaven of sweet hay and water to drink and deep straw to lie on, made ready earlier by John and Charlotte. The van moved forward and furniture was unloaded and left in the garden. The rain had not stopped.

Eddie came and spoke briefly: 'I've got Ma in there John. She'll need a chair.'

A weary lady was helped from the van and settled by the Aga. More things were unloaded and left in the garden. Rain blunted the clamour of sheep and barking dogs and the pitiful bleat of lambs. Eddie and two men were matching sheep with lambs separately transported. Rising above the turmoil a girl's voice shouted for someone or something called Banjo. There was no place for John and he returned to Ma and the Aga.

'Can I get you anything? Cook something?'

It was a long shot, she had a sizeable handbag which might have had eats, even a flask.

Ma was content, even sleepy, her voice a little slurred, the flask surely empty.

She told John she was 'Fine, thankyew'. They had stopped for a meal on the way. 'Fish an'chips, we had, really bewtiful, couldn't fault it. Lovely ...'

John could imagine. He went out again to tell Eddie about the heifer and why he was there. Eddie nodded an acceptance and went back to the sheep. His wife appeared, lugging a pretty large lamb: 'Needs his bottle, see?' In the kitchen with the raindrops glistening on his woolly coat the giant was fed.

So that was Banjo. And everybody, the whole gang, cows, sheep, lambs, Ma and Banjo, all were fed. John did not remember shooting the robin.

He was away long before daylight. It was a relief to be on the road again, traffic minimal and ahead breakfast. Somewhere, somehow he was going to eat. A layby cabin promised 'ALL DAY BREAKFASTS' but was boarded up. Later he had better luck and ate hugely; a Glaswegian producing thick bacon sandwiches saying 'Wha'se diet Jimmy?'

It was different after that. He began to see the funny side of it. After all the humping of damp furniture and decisions about who should sleep where, things had settled fairly peacefully until Banjo took to the stairs in search of company. And Banjo was one helluva heavy-footed lamb. In the end some cursing spoilsport put a stop to his gallop.

John had tried to leave quietly, tiptoeing through the heaped kitchen past dogs stretched on a sofa. All dogs liked John, these barely stirred, an old dog in an armchair moved a tired tail when spoken to. Getting his coat from the hall he had stumbled over a woolly heap and set Banjo off again: he could not help enjoying that. Payback! Giving Charlotte the flavour of it might be difficult, she was proud of the pale carpet, always busy with the vacuum and he had seen turds ... Better gloss over the burnt offering as well.

For the first time he thought of St Monans. What kind of a life was it going to be? There was the sea of course, and the house to lick into shape, places to visit ... and new people.

They would have to be careful and not talk too much about farming. He suspected it might be difficult: like old Falstaff, they would end up babbling of green fields.

ALSO BY IYANLA VANZANT

Tapping the Power Within: *A Path to Self-Empowerment for Women—20th Anniversary Edition*

Acts of Faith

Faith in the Valley: *Lessons for Women on the Journey to Peace*

Every Day I Pray: *Prayers for Awakening to the Grace of Inner Communion*

In the Meantime

One Day My Soul Just Opened Up: *40 Days and 40 Nights Toward Spiritual Strength and Personal Growth*

Until Today Cards: *A 50-Card Deck*

Tips for Daily Living Cards: *A 50-Card Deck*

The Value in the Valley: *A Black Woman's Guide Through Life's Dilemmas*

Please visit the distributor of SmileyBooks:

Hay House UK: **www.hayhouse.co.uk**
Hay House USA: **www.hayhouse.com**®
Hay House Australia: **www.hayhouse.com.au**
Hay House South Africa: **www.hayhouse.co.za**
Hay House India: **www.hayhouse.co.in**

BROKEN
FROM
PIECES